COME TO ME

A BIBLE STUDY FOR ALL
WHO THIRST FOR MORE.

September Year B to June Year C

Come to Me

A Bible Study for All
Who Thirst for More.

Gwen Meding

© 2006 by Gwen Meding. All rights reserved.

Pleasant Word (a division of WinePress Publishing, PO Box 428, Enumclaw, WA 98022) functions only as book publisher. As such, the ultimate design, content, editorial accuracy, and views expressed or implied in this work are those of the author.

No part of this publication may be reproduced, stored in a retrieval system or transmitted in any way by any means—electronic, mechanical, photocopy, recording or otherwise—without the prior permission of the copyright holder, except as provided by USA copyright law.

Unless otherwise noted, all Scriptures are taken from the *New Revised Standard Version* of the Bible, copyright @1989 by the National Council of the Churches of USA. Used by permission. All rights reserved.

Excerpts from the *New Jerusalem Bible,* Copyright (c) 1985 by Darton, Longman & Todd, Ltd. and Doubleday, a division of Random House, Inc. Reprinted with permission.

Excerpts from the *New American Bible* with Revised New Testament and Psalms Copyright @ 1991, 1986, 1970 Confraternity of Christian Doctrine, Inc., Washington, DC. Used with permission. All rights reserved. No portion of the *New American Bible* may be reprinted without permission in writing from the copyright holder.

Excerpts from *Catechism of the Catholic Church, Copyright @ Libreria Editrice Vaticana, 1992.* For the English Translations in Canada, Copyright @ Conacan Inc., 1994. All rights reserved. Used with permission of the Canadian Conference of Catholic Bishops. (www.cccbpublications.ca)

Scripture references are taken from Good News Bible, *Introduction to the Deutercanonical/Apocryphal Books* Copyright ©1992, American Bible Society Used by permission.

References are taken from *Handy Bible Dictionary and Concordance* by Zondervan Corporation, The. Copyright ©1983 by The Zondervan Corporation. Used by permission of The Zondervan Corporation.

Extract from *The Alpha Course Manual* published by Alpha International, first published 1993. Used by kind permission of Alpha International.

Joanie, E. Yoder, *Our Daily Bread,* Copyright 199 RBC Ministries, Grand Rapids, MI. Reprinted by permission. All rights reserved.

Brown, Raymond E; Fitzmeyer, Joseph A; Murphy, Roland E, New Jerome *Biblical Commentary,* 1st Edition @1990, Adapted by permission of Pearson Education, Inc., Upper Saddle River, NJ

Brown, Raymond E; Fitzmeyer, Joseph A; Murphy, Roland E, Jerome *Biblical Commentary, The,* 1st Edition @1969, Adapted by permission of Pearson Education, Inc., Upper Saddle River, NJ.

Albert Laisnez, *Setting the Stage,* Introduction to the first and second readings for Sundays and Solemnities, (Kwik Kopy Printing, 1998). used with kind permission.

ISBN 1-4141-0702-1
Library of Congress Catalog Card Number: 2006901824

DEDICATION

This book is dedicated to:

- My weekly Bible study group: Thank you for testing this study, for your encouragement, friendship and prayers. I am eternally grateful.
- My wonderful husband, Edward: Thank you for loving me and for the computer assistance.
- Fr. Brian: Thank you for checking each lesson and affirming my work.

May God richly bless you,
Gwen

Table of Contents

Foreword ix
How to Use This Bible Study xi

SECTION ONE: ORDINARY TIME
1. Twenty-Fourth Sunday of Ordinary Time - Year B 17
2. Triumph of The Cross 21
3. Twenty-Fifth Sunday of Ordinary Time - Year B 27
4. Twenty-Sixth Sunday of Ordinary Time - Year B 31
5. Twenty-Seventh Sunday of Ordinary Time - Year B 35
6. Twenty-Eighth Sunday of Ordinary Time - Year B 39
7. Twenty-Ninth Sunday of Ordinary Time - Year B 43
8. Thirtieth Sunday of Ordinary Time - Year B 47
9. Thirty-First Sunday of Ordinary Time - Year B 51
10. All Saints 55
11. All Souls Year B 61
12. Dedication of St. John Lateran 67
13. Thirty-Second Sunday of Ordinary Time - Year B 71
14. Thirty-Third Sunday of Ordinary Time - Year B 75
15. Christ the King Year B 79

SECTION TWO: ADVENT/CHRISTMAS
16. First Sunday of Advent Year C 87
17. Second Sunday of Advent Year C 91
18. Third Sunday of Advent Year C 95
19. Fourth Sunday of Advent Year C 99
20. Baptism of Our Lord Year C 103
21. Epiphany of the Lord Year C 109

SECTION THREE: ORDINARY TIME AFTER CHRISTMAS

22. Second Sunday of Ordinary Time Year C 117
23. Third Sunday of Ordinary Time Year C 121
24. Fourth Sunday of Ordinary Time Year C 125
25. Presentation of the Lord 129
26. Fifth Sunday of Ordinary Time Year C 135
27. Sixth Sunday of Ordinary Time Year C 139
28. Seventh Sunday of Ordinary Time Year C 143
29. Eighth Sunday of Ordinary Time Year C 147
30. Ninth Sunday of Ordinary Time Year C 151

SECTION FOUR: LENT

31. First Sunday of Lent Year C 159
32. Second Sunday of Lent Year C 163
33. Third Sunday of Lent Year C 169
34. Fourth Sunday Lent Year C 175
35. Fifth Sunday of Lent Year C 181
36. Passion Sunday Year C 185

SECTION FIVE: EASTER

37. Easter Sunday Year C 193
38. Second Sunday of Easter Divine Mercy Sunday Year C 197
39. Third Sunday of Easter Year C 201
40. Fourth Sunday of Easter Year C 207
41. Fifth Sunday of Easter Year C 211
42. Sixth Sunday of Easter Year C 215
43. Ascension Sunday Year C 221
44. Seventh Sunday of Easter (USA Only) Year C 227
45. Pentecost Sunday Year C 233
46. Trinity Sunday Year C 239
47. Body and Blood of Christ Year C 243

APPENDIX ONE: Deuterocanonical Books/Apocrypha 249
APPENDIX TWO: Definintion of the Word "World" as Used in Scripture 251
Endnotes 253

Foreword

The "Come" Bible study series is a valuable aid to group Bible study and a sure way to a deeper understanding of the Sunday readings. To study the readings in advance is to hear more clearly when they are proclaimed in the Eucharistic setting. Searching out the great web of scriptural parallels and allusions that Gwen Meding guides the reader through will mean a better comprehension of what the sacred author really intended to convey by what he wrote. To do this with friends as a group where all can share their own stories and their personal responses to the text is the way adults best learn. If you, or your group, are looking to achieve these goals, the "Come" Bible Study series will prove a very useful tool and guide.

—Fr. Brian Inglis csb, PhD

How to Use This Bible Study

The following ideas are notes and suggestions for this Bible study. I trust you will adapt and personalize the study to fit your group.

The "Come" Bible study series follows the three year Catholic lectionary (Year A, B, C). Traditionally a new lectionary year begins with Advent, at the end of November. But our Bible study begins in September; therefore, this study splits the lectionary year to accommodate this. Whatever date in the year your group begins, use the Bible study lesson applicable to the coming Sunday. The "Come" series includes:

Come and Rest—September Year A to June Year B
Come to Me—September Year B to June Year C
Come and Drink—September Year C to June Year A
Come to the Cross—Lenten Study on the Easter Vigil Readings

In the Catholic Lectionary, the following dates need to be watched. When Sunday falls on these dates, the feast day readings supersede the Sunday readings:

September 14	Triumph of the Cross supersedes the 24th Sunday.
November 1	All Saints Day supersedes the 31st Sunday of ordinary time.
November 2	All Souls Day supersedes the 31st Sunday of ordinary time.
November 9	Dedication of St John Lateran supersedes the 32nd Sunday.
February 2	Presentation of the Lord supersedes the 4th Sunday of ordinary time.

Each study is designed to take 2 to 2 ½ hours. If you have a large group, or your group discusses in-depth, you may want to do only one of the Sunday readings and use the next cycle for the second reading.

The "Come" series focuses on the first and second readings with a reference to the gospel. The history in the first reading relates to the gospel. This background broadens our understanding of the gospel. The second reading is always from the New Testament. Though this reading is not usually related to the gospel, it takes us through the main parts of the Epistles.

Come to Me

1. Study Format: Each week follows the same format. These are suggestions and can be adapted to your group.
     - **Opening Song**. A song is helpful to focus on the present moment and leave behind the hectic. Music can create an atmosphere of peace, reflection, and worship. This music may be taped.
     - **Opening Prayer**. Have someone open with a brief prayer inviting the Lord into this time; then encourage others to add their prayers. For example, "Lord, may we be aware of your presence here tonight. We give you permission to work in our hearts. Bless our families. I invite everyone to add your own prayer." Close by reading together the opening prayer given in the study.
     - **Group Guidelines**. Reviewing these weekly builds trust and sets boundaries and expectations. All are accepted where they are today and encouraged to grow in their faith.
     - **Setting the Stage**. This portion is taken, with permission, from Fr. Albert Laisnez's book of the same title. It gives the historical background and setting for the readings. In the original, "parish" and "parishioner" are used. I have changed these to "church" and "Christian" for the Come series.
     - **First Reading**. Read aloud twice. Listen for the word, the phrase, or the idea that stands out to you. Briefly discuss as a group.
     - **Exploring Further**. Through a question format, the reading is broken apart so we can see how corresponding Scriptures and past events are linked. We discover how God's promises in the Old Testament are fulfilled in the New. Over the year we come to see the great scriptural themes woven from Genesis to Revelation. As we hear God's word it transforms our minds and hearts. We grow in knowledge and in faith. The Scriptures used in this section are mainly taken from the cross reference Scriptures in *The New Jerusalem Bible*, 1985—Doubleday Company.
     - **Reflection**. We now take the truths of the Scriptures just discussed and apply them to our lives with the help of reflection questions.
     - **Optional Exercise** before the second reading. There is an optional exercise between the first and second readings to give participants a chance to share something about their week. We found this time draws groups closer. As needs are made known, the group has opportunities to help one another. A time limit is needed. Some groups may want to do this exercise at the beginning.
     - **Second Reading**. This follows the same format as the First Reading.
     - **Closing Prayer**. Feel free to do intercessory prayer at the end, or add a song, or whatever the group wants.

2. Using the Bible tips:
     - The group may have a variety of Scripture translations. This adds richness and understanding, and clarifies the meaning. *Please note that the numbering of the verses varies in some translations.* When there is a discrepancy in numbering, the NRSV translation is the standard used for this study. To clarify when there is a discrepancy, the NRSV verse will be noted and the verse in other translations will be in parentheses. Example: Isaiah 64:8 (or verse 7). The numbering of verses varies in parts of Isaiah, Job, Psalms, Hosea, and the end of Malachi. All Bible quotes, unless otherwise stated, are from the NRSV: Catholic Edition, copyright 1993.

How to Use This Study

- When one question has several Scriptures, designating people to each look up one Scripture helps if time is a factor.
- Some people may not feel comfortable finding the Scripture references in the "Exploring Further" section. I encourage you to use the index and to assist each other in locating Scriptures. Reassure those who may be intimidated because they are unfamiliar with a Bible. We are all learning.
- When a Scripture verse is long this study uses a reference letter "a" to indicate the first part and a "b" to indicate the second part. For example, Isaiah 43:1 could be divided into Isaiah 43:1a and 43:1b for discussion purposes.

STUDY GROUP GUIDELINES

LISTEN	I will not interrupt, teach, or lecture. I will give everyone an opportunity to speak. I will not chatter on or dominate the conversation.
RESPECT	I will allow everyone to share at their own comfort level. I will not make judgmental or critical remarks. I will not give unsolicited advice.
CONFIDENTIALITY	I will keep what is said in the group, in the group. I will not share what is not mine to share.
PARTICIPATION	I will participate in the discussion. I will remember the group is never the same without me. My insights and experiences are valuable to the group.

SECTION ONE

ORDINARY TIME

This Bible study begins in September. This time of the church year is referred to as ordinary time. Ordinary time will continue until the Feast of Christ the King, near the end of November, and it is followed by Advent. Ordinary time or routine time is the best environment for spiritual growth. *This is the time to develop daily practices and habits that build a foundation of faith and a relationship with God.*

The highlight of an athlete's life may be the Olympics or the championship game, but it is the daily habits and practices that make the highlight game possible. The following excerpt is a paraphrase of a story told at a parish mission that illustrates the importance of making good use of ordinary time in our faith life.

> A concert pianist told his students to practice so well that if their own strength failed, they would be able to carry on out of habit. Just before a sold out concert was to begin, the pianist suffered a stroke that left him blind and weak. Those around him wanted to cancel the performance, but he said, "No." With assistance, he was led to the piano. All his years of practice prepared him for this moment. He played flawlessly for his last appearance. Because of the years of daily practice, habit took over when his own strength failed.

A regular routine of our faith practices and prayer habits builds a firm foundation that can be relied on when our own strength fails. *We are building a relationship with God that prepares us for whatever is to come.* The ordinary seasons of our life are important. Use them wisely.

I play the notes as they are written...
but it is God
Who makes the music.

(J. S. Bach)

CHAPTER 1
Twenty-Fourth Sunday of Ordinary Time – Year B

Opening Song
Opening Prayer

Open in prayer and invite everyone to add their own prayer. Close together: "Lord, give peace and courage to those who wait on you. Creator and guide, hear the prayers of your servants. Amen."

Review Study Guidelines

First Reading   Isaiah 50:5-9

Setting the Stage

The first reading is from the book of the prophet Isaiah. These words were spoken about 540 years before Jesus, and this is known as the Third Song of the Suffering Servant. This servant is probably the writer himself; he has been rejected by his people as he tries to help them during their exile in Babylon. His life becomes a symbol of the Hebrew suffering and has become an image of Jesus. Through these words God our Father describes *what it sometimes costs to speak for Him.*

Read the first reading aloud. Reread this Scripture.
What word, phrase, or idea stands out for you?

COME TO ME

Exploring Further

1. What does God do for the servant and how does the servant respond in Isaiah 50:4-5?

2. What do we learn about turning our ear to the Lord in Proverbs 2:1-6?

3. What revelation is the reason why the disciples and believers today are obedient to Jesus as recorded in Mark 8:27-30, Sunday's gospel?

4. How is the servant treated when obedient to the Lord in Isaiah 50:6?

5. How is Jesus to be treated for his obedience to his Father in Mark 8:31-33, Sunday's gospel?

6. What life does Jesus call his followers to in Mark 8:34-38, Sunday's gospel?

7. What is the servant's hope and what is his response to the abuse in Isaiah 50:7?

8. How has God prepared his prophet for abuse and what is the prophet still called to do in Ezekiel 3:8-11?

9. What is the servant's boast and challenge to his abusers in Isaiah 50:8-10?

10. How do the following Scriptures support the servant's confidence in God?
    Isaiah 51:12, 14
    Isaiah 54:17
    Romans 8:33-39

Reflection

1. In what ways do you seek to hear God's voice and are obedient to it? In what ways do you avoid "listening" or are rebellious or disobedient or lazy when you do hear?

2. As a church community and a people of God, locally and worldwide, where do you see signs of listening and obeying God's word happening? Where do you see we need to improve our listening skills and obedience?

3. In the world today, what people and groups are speaking against injustice? What are the results or consequences? Consider your life; how you live, what you do, what you speak. What opportunities do you have to address unjust situations? Do you do so? Why or why not? How is living and working toward justice intertwined with the whole gospel message and an important part of what we are called to speak?

Twenty-Fourth Sunday of Ordinary Time – Year B

4. The servant in Isaiah 50:8-10 make these promises his foundation to stand on: "The Lord helps me, I will not be disgraced," "I know that I shall not be put to shame; he who vindicates me is near," "It is the Lord God who helps me," and, "Let him who walks in the dark and who has no light trust in the name of the Lord and rely on his God." What situation are you in (or have been in) where you need to have confidence in God's promises despite the pain and disappointment? How do you make these promises real, a solid foundation to stand on, in spite of present circumstances?

Optional Exercise before the second reading: Have each person in the group briefly tell something of their past week or of an event anticipated in the coming week. This could be a time to share a triumph, a trial, or a need.

Second Reading　　　James 2:14-18

Setting the Stage

The next reading is from the letter of James. This book was written by a Jewish Christian to other Jewish Christians living outside Palestine about 40 years after the resurrection of Jesus. Through these words God our Father tells us *how we can know if we have real faith or not.*

Read the second reading aloud. Reread this Scripture.
What word, phrase, or idea stands out for you?

Exploring Further

1. What is the definite result of faith according to James 2:14-17?

2. Consider the following Scriptures. How are love, faith, and works connected?
   Matthew 7:16-20
   1 Corinthians 13:3
   Galatians 5:16
   1 John 3:17

3. How important does God consider "good works" according to Matthew 25:41-45?

4. How would you reconcile these two Scriptures?
   James 2:18
   Romans 3:28.

Come to Me

Reflection

1. There are two traps that we can fall into. The first trap is trying to do good things to earn God's love and salvation. Paul stresses that salvation is a free gift to be received through Jesus Christ and cannot be earned. The second trap is giving intellectual assent only. James emphasizes true biblical faith transforms (a conversion of the heart) and the fruit is good works and a relationship of love with God and others. Have there been times in your life when you were in one of these two traps? Which one? How did you move out?

2. The church has a long history and in-depth teaching on social justice. I recommend you read in the *Catechism of the Catholic Church* #2419 to #2449 to get a basic idea of this teaching.
   Catechism #2459: Man is himself the author, centre, and goal of all economic and social life. The decisive point of the social question is that goods created by God for everyone should in fact reach everyone in accordance with justice and with the help of charity.
   Catechism #2460: By means of his labour man participates in the work of creation. Work united to Christ can be redemptive.[1]
   - Do you think biblical faith (conversion) is necessary before people work for justice and help the "poorest of the poor"? Why or why not?
   - What priority are justice issues to you?
   - Do you consider your talents, wages, and job benefits as belonging to you alone or something to be shared? Why or why not?
   - Do you consider your job and work as a gift? A participation in creation? A basic right? Something you have no choice in? Boring? Inconvenient? Other? Why?

Closing Prayer

"Lord, let your words influence our thoughts and actions. Help us be just and generous. Amen."

CHAPTER 2
TRIUMPH OF THE CROSS
ONLY WHEN SUNDAY FALLS ON SEPTEMBER 14TH

OPENING SONG
OPENING PRAYER

Open in prayer and invite everyone to add their own prayer. Close together: "Lord Jesus, may we always glory in your cross, for your are our salvation, our life and our resurrection. Your cross has saved us and made free. Amen."

REVIEW STUDY GUIDELINES

First Reading Numbers 21:4-9

Setting the Stage

The first reading is from the book of Numbers. It describes the escape of the Hebrews from slavery in Egypt in 1300 BC. They go through the Red Sea and into the Sinai Desert and eventually come to Edom, an area south of the Dead Sea. It is a hot, dry journey and the people complain even about the "manna," their desert food. The writer is a person of deep faith who interprets all events, both good and bad, as coming from God, including the disaster that follows the complaints. The remedy provided seems very strange. We need to focus on the faith and trust in the hearts of the people as they do what is asked of them. *This is an appropriate reading for this feast of the Cross of Jesus, for we too "look with faith and trust" on it, the sign of our healing and peace.*

Read the first reading aloud. Reread this Scripture.
What word, phrase, or idea stands out for you?

Come to Me

Exploring Further

1. What are the people doing in Numbers 21:4-5?

2. What is the temperament of the people from the start of the great exodus in Exodus 14:10-16?

3. The people are complaining about the food. How are they cared for in the desert?
   Exodus 16:11-15
   Exodus 17:2-6
   Deuteronomy 8:15-16

4. What is the consequence of the people's complaining against God and Moses in Numbers 21:6?

5. After experiencing the consequence of complaining, what do the people do and how does Moses respond in Numbers 21:7?

6. What do the following Scriptures tell us about the role of Moses?
   Exodus 32:7-14, 30-32
   Numbers 11:1-2
   Numbers 13:30–14:3, 11-24

7. What is the consequence of sin for all people according to Romans 6:23?

8. Who is the mediator that Moses is "a type of" or prefigures in 1 Timothy 2:5?

9. When Moses intercedes what does God tell him to do? What will result in Numbers 21:8-9?

10. What does Jesus compare to the bronze serpent? What does he say will result, according to John 3:14-16, Sunday's gospel?

11. How is the bronze serpent misused according to 2 Kings 18:1-4?

12. What truth is stated in Wisdom 16:5-8? (See appendix one.)

13. What truth is stated in the following Scriptures?
    Deuteronomy 9:6
    Titus 3:5

14. What is the triumph of the cross according to John 3:16-17?

Triumph of The Cross (Only When Sunday Falls on September 14th)

Reflection

1. The Israelites complained about the water, the food, Moses and Aaron's position of authority, and how powerful the enemy was. How is complaining like a poisonous snake?

2. Do you know someone who shows gratitude, even for small things? What effect does that have on you?

3. The Israelites complaining against God and Moses is severely punished in today's reading. Another time they start by complaining then proceed to worship a golden calf and to rebel against Moses and his authority. Each time the consequences are severe. Do you think there are serious consequences to complaining, worshiping idols, rebelling, and other sin today? Why or why not?

4. After the disciplining, the people repent and turn back to God. Has a negative consequence to a choice you have made resulted in your return to God? Explain.

5. God heals the Israelites when they look at the bronze serpent, a reminder of their sin. Over time they begin to worship the instrument of healing rather than the healer. When God uses a person, a group, or an object to bless and heal us, what danger is there of lifting up the instrument rather than giving glory to God?

Optional Exercise before the second reading. Have each person in the group briefly tell something of their past week or of an event anticipated in the coming week. This could be a time to share a triumph, trial or a need.

Second Reading   Philippians 2:6-11

Setting the Stage

The next reading is from the letter of St. Paul to the church at Philippi, northern Greece. He is writing from a prison, perhaps in western Israel, about 30 years after the resurrection of Jesus. The Philippian church sent help to Paul and he writes to thank them and to encourage them in their faith. This reading is actually a quote from an early Christian hymn. Note: "Under the earth" refers to the place of the dead. *God our Father through these words is showing us what comes after the cross.*

Read the second reading aloud. Reread this Scripture.
What word, phrase, or idea stands out for you?

Come to Me

Exploring Further

1. What does Paul beg of the Philippians in Philippians 2:1-2?

2. What should be avoided and what should we try to do according to Philippians 2:3-5?

3. What does Jesus do according to Philippians 2:6-7?

4. What position does Jesus not cling to?
   John 1:1-3
   Hebrews 1:3

5. What does Jesus' becoming human cost him, according to the following Scriptures?
   John 5:18
   John 10:33
   Matthew 20:28
   Romans 8:3

6. To what extent does Jesus humble himself in Philippians 2:8?

7. What is the result of Jesus' action for us according to John 3:14-15, Sunday's gospel?

8. What does the obedience of Jesus cost him according to Matthew 26:36-39?

9. What promise is given to those who humble themselves in Matthew 23:12?

10. How does the cross triumph according to Philippians 2:9-10?

11. What title does the resurrection give Jesus in Philippians 2:11?

12. What possible responses to the death and resurrection of Jesus are suggested in 1 Corinthians 1:23-25?

Reflection

1. Avalanches, volcanoes, tornados, and raging floods are four powerful natural forces. What powerful natural force have you experienced?

2. "The cross of Jesus is the most powerful spiritual force in the universe. This single act has won forgiveness for every sin that has ever been committed, has defeated the devil and his minions that attempt to control our lives, and has ripped the veil that separated heaven from earth and revealed a new and living way to the Father. Have you seen a sin pattern exploded as you turned to the Lord

Triumph of The Cross (Only When Sunday Falls on September 14th)

for help? Have you seen a relationship that seemed beyond saving turn around?"[2] Where have you experienced the power of the cross in your life? What situation in your life do you want to take to the cross? What might you be clinging to or grasping for or trying to control in your life that God is asking you to let go of at the cross?

3. The Christian life is full of paradox; dying to receive life, emptying self to be filled, humbling self to be exalted, the first shall be last, deny self and serve others, and many others. Jesus set the example for this way of living and it often goes against secular culture. How would you describe your desire and motivation to model your life on that of Jesus the Christ? What gives you hope, inspiration, and a hunger to claim and live the victory won for you on the cross?

Closing Prayer

Lord, by your cross you have redeemed the world. We give you honor, glory, and praise for leading us to life. Amen

CHAPTER 3
Twenty-Fifth Sunday of Ordinary Time – Year B

Opening Song
Opening Prayer

Open in prayer and invite everyone to add their own prayer. Close together: "Lord, you are the upholder of our lives. Help us not to grow weary or lose heart. Amen."

Review Study Guidelines

First Reading Wisdom 2:12, 17-20 (See appendix one.)

Setting the Stage

The first reading is from the book of Wisdom. This book is written only about 50 years or so before Jesus, in Alexandria, Egypt, to encourage Jews loyal to their faith. Their lives are a silent protest against the "godless," the unbelievers, and against those Jews who have given up the practice of their faith. Through these words, God our Father tells us *the price Jesus paid, and also the price we will pay when we stand up for what is right.*

Read the first reading aloud. Reread this Scripture.
What word, phrase, or idea stands out for you?

Come to Me

Exploring Further

1. How do the godless see the upright man in Wisdom 2:12-16?

2. Whose son does the upright man claim to be and how are they going to test this truth in Wisdom 2:17-18?

3. What does the son Jesus say will happen to him in Mark 9:30-32, Sunday's gospel?

4. How is David jeered in Psalm 22:7-8? (or verse 8-9)

5. How is Jesus mocked in Luke 23:39?

6. How do the prophet and Jesus respond to the mocking?
   Isaiah 53:7
   Matthew 27:13-14

7. How do they plan to test the upright man in Wisdom 2:19-20?

8. This passage is considered prophetic by a number of Fathers of the Church. What similarities do Wisdom 2:18-20 and Matthew 27:28-31, 41-44 have?

9. How is the upright person in every age to stand firm according to Hebrews 12:3?

10. How does Jesus say the upright person should act in Mark 9:33-37, Sunday's gospel?

Reflection

1. A person living a simple, holy, and faithful life may inspire some people to do likewise and others may be convicted and react with jealousy, gossip, pride, defensiveness, cruelty, and rejection. Why do you think this happens? Can you think of a time someone else's life caused you to want to live or act that way, or caused you to be unkind?

2. One time I heard a deacon from the United States tell a story from his life. When he was first ordained a deacon he was married and had six children. He was assigned to a parish where the priest did not want a deacon. He was told he could do no ministry in that parish. Every Sunday he and his family went to church and were ignored by everyone. They were ridiculed and scorned in the community. This deacon drove outside his diocese and did some work in another area, but in his area he was not allowed. During this time of persecution the deacon restored a small chapel in the country that had been abandoned and prayed for the community, surrendering his suffering to God. This continued for a long time.

Twenty-Fifth Sunday of Ordinary Time – Year B

On confirmation Sunday the bishop was present and saying mass. The bishop was aware of the situation and on the way out of mass, he stopped at the deacon's pew, took him in his arms, and wept. The deacon said that at the bishop's action of love, conviction came upon the people. Many wept. They began to say it was wrong to treat anyone this way, let alone a man of God. Many asked his family's forgiveness. Eventually he was allowed to minister in that area. He opened a Bible school and there was a renewal in the area. The deacon said that by Jesus' wounds we are healed (Isaiah 53:5) and when our suffering is surrendered to God, others are healed.

Can you think of a situation where peace, gentleness, and mercy won out over power and cruelty? Who, in our day or in the past, lived this way and with what results?

3. How does reflecting on the hostility Jesus endured and the victory He gained keep you from growing weary or losing heart? How did Mary the mother of Jesus deal with suffering in her life?

Optional Exercise before the second reading. Have each person in the group briefly tell something of their past week or of an event anticipated in the coming week. This could be a time to share a triumph, a trial, or a need.

Second Reading — James 3:16-4:3

Setting the Stage

The second reading is from the letter of James. This is written by a Jewish Christian to other Jewish Christians living outside Palestine about 40 years after the resurrection of Jesus. Through these words God our Father speaks about three things:
1. What is wisdom?
2. Why do people not get along with each other?
3. How should we pray?

Read the second reading aloud. Reread this Scripture.
What word, phrase, or idea stands out for you?

Exploring Further

1. What is the fruit of envy and selfish ambition mentioned in James 3:16?

2. What are the characteristics of wisdom from above in James 3:17?

3. How do the characteristics of wisdom from above compare to how love is described in the following verses?
Romans 12:9-11, 18
1 Corinthians 13:4-7

4. When peace is sown, what is the harvest in James 3:18?

5. What else produces this harvest according to Hebrews 12:10-11?

6. What causes disputes among us?
James 4:1-2a
Galatians 5:17
1 Peter 2:11

7. What common problems with prayer does James mention in 4:2b-3?

8. What competes for our devotion according to James 4:4?

Reflection

1. Consider the standard of living we have in North America. How does our wanting more possessions, more money, and more pleasure affect third world countries?

2. Consider your last quarrel or conflict with someone. What desires of the flesh can you identify that rose up in you? Were you able to use any of the wisdom from above which is: pure, peaceable, gentle, willing to yield, full of mercy and good fruits, without a trace of partiality or hypocrisy at this time? Considering James 3:17, how might you respond differently another time?

3. Common problems in prayer that James mentions are not asking, asking for wrong things, or asking for wrong reasons. What would examples of each of these be? What are examples and characteristics of true prayer?

4. What are examples of things in this world people often look for to meet their needs rather than looking to God? God is a jealous God who want our hearts devoted to him and look to him to meet our needs. How can we be sure our love and devotion is to God and not to things? How can we continue to grow in our devotion and love of God?

Closing Prayer

Create in us a clean heart, Lord, that we may be wholly devoted to you. Amen.

CHAPTER 4
Twenty-Sixth Sunday of Ordinary Time – Year B

Opening Song
Opening Prayer

Open in prayer and invite everyone to add their own prayer. Close together: "Lord, your ways are perfect and they give us joy and refreshment. Help us to see where you are working in our midst. Amen."

Review Study Guidelines

First Reading — Numbers 11:16-17, 25-29

Setting the Stage

The first reading is from the book of Numbers. We read about the journey of the Hebrew people from slavery in Egypt, through the Sinai Desert, to freedom in Palestine about 1300 BC. To lead them is too big a job for one man, so Moses listens to the advice given by his father-in-law. We hear now "the rest of the story." Note two important features in the life of the Hebrews in their desert journey:

1. A large "tent" is set up outside the secular campsite; it houses the Ark of the Covenant—the sacred wooden box containing the two stone tablets on which are written the Ten Commandments.
2. There is a cloud guiding them by day. This cloud is a symbol of the divine presence. Through these words, God our Father shows us that *he is not limited to only one way when he wants to do something for us, his people.*

COME TO ME

Read the first reading aloud. Reread this Scripture.
What word, phrase, or idea stands out for you?

Exploring Further

1. In the verses preceding today's reading, what pressures, stresses, and state of mind is Moses in according to Numbers 11:10-15?

2. What advice does Jethro give to Moses in order to reduce the pressure of governing this people in Exodus 18:21-26?

3. How does God respond to Moses' request to die because the burden is too great, in Numbers 11:16-17?

4. How does God confirm the leadership of the seventy elders chosen in Numbers 11:25?

5. What happens to two men back at the main camp in Numbers 11:26?

6. What is Joshua's reaction to this occurrence in Numbers 11:28?

7. What is Moses' response in Numbers 11:29?

8. What is Jesus' response to a similar situation in Mark 9:38-41, Sunday's gospel?

Reflection

1. How have you experienced discouragement in leadership (at home or in a group) because of complaining people and/or by carrying too great a burden? What happened to help you out?

2. We hear concern in our church today about too great a burden on too few shoulders as fewer people are choosing vocations to be priests and religious. What effect has the shortage of religious caused? How are lay people caring for and nurturing the life of your parish in the midst of this shortage?

3. When you see that the Spirit touches those around you using people outside of priests and religious, or by groups you are not a part of, or by other denominations, can you recognize and celebrate this or do you feel a need to defend the church or your own groups? Why or why not?

Optional Exercise before the second reading. Have each person in the group briefly tell something of their past week or of an event anticipated in the coming week. This could be a time to share a triumph, a trial, or a need.

Twenty-Sixth Sunday of Ordinary Time – Year B

Second Reading — James 5:1-6

Setting the Stage

The next reading is from the letter of James. This is written by a Jewish Christian to other Jewish Christians living outside Palestine about 40 years after the resurrection of Jesus. He writes very harsh words to people who are rich. Through these words *God our Father warns us about placing too much importance on our money, clothes, and other material possessions.*

Read the second reading aloud. Reread this Scripture.
What word, phrase, or idea stands out for you?

Exploring Further

1. What warning regarding riches is given in the following verses?
   James 5:1-3
   Luke 6:24-25
   Proverbs 11:4, 28

2. What kind of treasure should we seek according to the following Scriptures?
   Romans 12:20-21
   Matthew 6:19-21
   Sirach 29:8-13 (or 11-16) See appendix one

3. What injustice is spoken of in James 5:4?

4. Compare James 5:4, written in 40 AD, with Deuteronomy 24:14-15 written around 1300 BC. What does this say to you regarding how important this message of justice is to God and the consistency of this message?

5. What is the attitude of the rich in James 5:5-6?

6. What does Jesus say our attitude toward righteousness should be in Mark 9:42-48, Sunday's gospel?

7. How does this compare to the attitude expressed in Wisdom 2:10-12?

8. Often we wonder why the wicked flourish. How is this question so eloquently asked in Jeremiah 12:1-3?

9. When will righteousness flourish according to James 5: 7-8?

10. What do you discover regarding the love of money in 1 Timothy 6:10?

Reflection

1. The creation of wealth can be a virtue; the hoarding of it is not. The Church's teaching is clear. "The goods of creation are destined for the entire human race. The right of private property does not abolish the universal destination of goods."[3] We are to be stewards of what we possess and wealth is to be shared. Are money and riches in themselves wrong? Why or why not? What is the danger of money and riches? If our heart and treasure is in seeking God, how will we use our money and riches as a result?

2. Where money is concerned, it can be easy for us to justify and deceive ourselves. What might be guidelines or fruits we could use to judge if we are using our resources wisely?

3. Can you think of examples of unjust labor practices in our country? In other countries? With the development of strong unions, in what ways is it possible to have unjust employees?

Closing Prayer

The ordinances of the Lord are true and righteous altogether. By them your servant is warned; in keeping them there is great reward. Lord, cleanse us from hidden fault and make us a holy people. Amen.

CHAPTER 5
Twenty-Seventh Sunday of Ordinary Time – Year B

Opening Song
Opening Prayer

Open in prayer and invite everyone to add their own prayer. Close together: "Lord, you are the creator of all. May we be aware of your blessings all the days of our lives. Amen."

Review Study Guidelines

First Reading   Genesis 2:7-8b, 18-24

Setting the Stage

The first reading is from different portions of chapter two of the book of Genesis. It is very important to understand that the first eleven chapters of this book, dealing with the creation of the universe and the very beginnings of the human race, are not intended to be taken literally. The Bible is not a science book. These chapters are powerful poetic presentations that God our Father uses to teach us *the truth* about our world and our lives, and he uses striking images to answer questions like these:

1. Are humans and their world the result of chance or did "Someone" make plans for them?
2. Are human beings made to be alone or are they made to be in relationships with others?
3. Are women and men made of the same stuff; do we yearn for the same things?

Read the first reading aloud. Reread this Scripture.
What word, phrase, or idea stands out for you?

Come to Me

Exploring Further

1. From what substance is man formed and what gives us life according to Genesis 2:7?

2. What truth about life do the following Scriptures teach us?
   Job 33:4
   Psalm 104:29-30
   Ezekiel 37:1, 5-10, 14
   John 20:21-23

3. What truth is revealed in Genesis 2:18?

4. How are the creation of woman, and man's response, described in Genesis 2: 21-23?

5. What significance does this have for men and women in terms of equality, unity, partnership, intimacy, and oneness?

6. How is the institution of marriage established? What three actions must be taken and in what order according to Genesis 2: 24?

7. What does Jesus teach in Mark 10:2-10, Sunday's gospel?

Reflection

1. What circumstance have you experienced in your life that has been like "the valley of dry bones" or "dry as dust"? How did God breathe life into you in this circumstance?

2. When we enter marriage we first need to leave—leave parents, friends, work, or sports and so on as a first priority. What did you have to leave (or would have to leave) to put your spouse first? Was this easy, difficult, a process, something you never realized, other?
   If you are a religious, what did you have to leave in order to enter your covenant relationship? Was this easy, difficult, a process, other?
   If you are single, what important life choice caused you to leave behind something? What effect did this have on you?

3. According to the *Funk and Wagnall's Dictionary,* to "cleave" means: to stick fast; adhere; to be faithful to; fusion of. What images do these words portray to you? What do these words say to you regarding marriage?

4. In God's plan for marriage we are to leave, cleave, and *then* become one flesh.
   Do you think this order make sense? Why or why not?

Twenty-Seventh Sunday of Ordinary Time – Year B

What do you think are the results when this order is followed?

What do you think are the results when this order is not followed?

5. "The church holds the exchange of consent between the spouses, free of coercion or grave external fear, to be the indispensable element that "makes the marriage." If consent is lacking there is no marriage."[4] 'For a marriage to be truly valid (with the Catholic understanding of covenant) both parties must be capable of such a commitment, fully aware, and freely giving consent. Sometimes one of these conditions is not present. In such a case there never was a valid marriage bond from the beginning. One or both parties may not have been capable of full consent for a number of personal reasons, or there may have been undue external pressure. An annulment process is aimed at establishing that the marriage bond was invalid from the beginning.'[5]

How is the annulment process faithful to God's revelation of the indissolubility of marriage and also compassionate?

What are possible examples of situations that may make a marriage invalid?

How does annulment differ from divorce and how can we show compassion to people in both situations?

Optional Exercise before the second reading. Have each person in the group briefly tell something of their past week or of an event anticipated in the coming week. This could be a time to share a triumph, a trial, or a need.

Second Reading   Hebrews 2:9-11

Setting the Stage

The second reading is from the letter to the Hebrews. This is written by a Jewish Christian to other Jewish Christians about 40 years after the resurrection of Jesus. Through these words, God our Father tells us *the price Jesus paid to be our Leader, our "Pioneer" in faith.*

Read this reading aloud. Reread this Scripture.

What word, phrase, or idea stands out for you?

Exploring Further

1. Why is Christ glorified and who benefits from this according to Hebrews 2:9?

2. What do we discover about the existence of all things?
   Hebrews 2:10a
   1 Corinthians 8:6

3. What name is Jesus given?
   Hebrews 2:10b
   Acts 3:15

4. Because God rescues David, what does he tell his brothers and sisters in Psalm 22:22?

5. Who is the one who sanctifies and who is sanctified in Hebrews 2:11?

6. What also sanctifies us according to John 17:19?

Reflection

1. To "sanctify" means to make holy; set aside for God's service. Through Jesus' suffering, death and resurrection we have been made holy and set aside for God's service. What does this mean to you? We are holy because of Jesus. How does this change the ordinary things we do each day?

2. Through Jesus Christ we are one family—brothers and sisters to all believers. What does being part of this large family mean to you?

3. What has Jesus done in your life (sanctified) that you are grateful for?

Closing Prayer

Father, your love for us surpasses all our hopes and desires. Continue to purify us and lead us ever closer to you and to one another. Amen.

CHAPTER 6
Twenty-Eighth Sunday of Ordinary Time – Year B

Opening Song
Opening Prayer

Open in prayer and invite everyone to add their own prayer. Close together: "Lord, our ever present help, teach us to seek you that we may gain a wise heart. Amen."

Review Study Guidelines

First Reading Wisdom 7:7-11 (See appendix one).

Setting the Stage

The first reading is from the book of Wisdom. This book is written only about 50 years or so before Jesus, in Alexandria, Egypt, to encourage Jews living in an unbelieving society to hold on to their faith. We hear the "spirit of wisdom" being described as a beautiful, attractive woman. Through these words, God our Father tells us of the *importance of wisdom and how we can become wise.*

Read the first reading aloud. Reread this Scripture.
What word, phrase, or idea stands out for you?

Exploring Further

1. What does Solomon do to gain understanding and wisdom in Wisdom 7:7?

COME TO ME

2. What do we discover about seeking God and wisdom?
   Proverbs 2:3-11
   Matthew 6:33

3. Why is Solomon given wisdom? What else does he receive in 1 Kings 3:6-9, 12-13?

4. What value does Solomon place on wisdom in Wisdom 7:8-9?

5. How is the value of wisdom expressed in Job 28:17-18?

6. What struggle with riches does the young man have in Mark 10:17-22, Sunday's gospel?

7. What does Jesus say regarding wealth in Mark 10:23-27?

8. What will be rewarded according to Mark 10:28-31?

9. What does Solomon do with the wisdom he receives according to Wisdom 7:13?

Reflection

1. When you think of a wise person, who comes to mind and how have they influenced your life?

2. How important is wisdom to you? How in your life are you seeking wisdom "as though it were buried treasure"? In what ways does "seeking" take a choice and hard work?

3. What are some examples of how God's wisdom differs from worldly wisdom?

Optional Exercise before the second reading. Have each person in the group briefly tell something of their past week or of an event anticipated in the coming week. This could be a time to share a triumph, a trial, or a need.

Twenty-Eighth Sunday of Ordinary Time – Year B

Second Reading   Hebrews 4:12-13

Setting the Stage

The second reading is from the letter to the Hebrews. This is written by a Jewish Christian to other Jewish Christians about 40 years or so after the resurrection of Jesus. Here is a powerful, poetic description of *what happens when the Word of God Our Father is proclaimed and read in faith.*

Read the second reading. Reread this Scripture.
What word, phrase, or idea stands out for you?

Exploring Further

1. What action verbs are used to describe the Word of God in Hebrews 4:12?

2. What happens when a person receives the Word of God according to 1 Peter 1:23?

3. To what is the Word of God compared in Hebrews 4:12?

4. What is described as a sword in the following Scriptures? Explain.
    Isaiah 49:2
    Ephesians 6:17
    Revelation 1:16

5. What is the job of this "sword" according to the remainder of Hebrews 4:12?

6. What is said about the "sword" in John 12:48?

7. What do we learn about the "word" in John 1:1?

8. What do we find out about God's knowledge in Hebrews 4:13?

9. What do the following Scriptures say about what God sees and knows?
    Job 34:21-22
    Psalm 33:13-15
    Wisdom 1:6

10. What did the Thessalonians do when they heard the Word of God in 1 Thessalonians 2:13?

11. What does Jesus discern in the heart of the rich young man and how does the young man respond in Mark 10:20-22, Sunday's gospel?

12. What is the prayer expressed in Psalm 19:13-15?

Reflection

1. According to Hebrews four, the Word of God is living and active. What signs indicate the Word of God is living and active in your study group?

2. "With the incisiveness of a surgeon's knife, God's Word reveals who we are and what we are not. It penetrates the core of our moral and spiritual life. It discerns what is within us, both good and evil."[6] Do you desire God to reveal what is in your heart to you? Why or why not?

3. How do you respond when God reveals something hidden in your heart?

4. Nothing is hidden from God. He knows about everyone and everything. We cannot hide or get lost from God. Does this comfort or disturb you? Why?

Closing Prayer

Who can detect their errors? Cleanse me from hidden faults. Then I shall be blameless and innocent of great transgression. Let the words of my mouth and the meditation of my heart be acceptable to you, O Lord, my rock and my redeemer (Psalm 19:12, 13b, 14).

CHAPTER 7
Twenty-Ninth Sunday of Ordinary Time – Year B

Opening Song
Opening Prayer

Open in prayer and invite everyone to add their own prayer. Close together: "Lord, God Almighty, be our source of inspiration and power as we proclaim you to all people. Be our strength and joy in serving you as faithful followers of Christ. Amen."

Review Study Guidelines

First Reading   Isaiah 53:4, 10-11

Setting the Stage

The first reading is from the book of the prophet Isaiah. These words are first spoken around 540 BC. when the Hebrew people are deported to Babylon. We hear about a certain "servant of the Lord" and what he goes through in trying to bring encouragement to these people in exile. The writer has such deep faith that, for him, everything that happens, good and bad, joy and pain, all comes from God. *Through these words God our Father tells us how he will bring good out of the evil and pain of this world, especially in the life and death of Jesus, his Son.*

Read the first reading aloud. Reread this Scripture.
What word, phrase, or idea stands out for you?

Come to Me

Exploring Further

1. Whose suffering and sorrow is the servant carrying in Isaiah 53:4a?

2. What do the people think is happening because the servant is suffering in Isaiah 53:4b?

3. What effect does the suffering of our leader Jesus have in Hebrews 2:10?

4. What does God choose to do according to Isaiah 53:10a?

5. What is the result of the servant's pain?
   Isaiah 53b
   Psalm 22:30 (or 31)

6. What does God choose to do according to John 10:14-18?

7. What is the result according to Romans 5:18?

8. After the servant suffered, not for any guilt of his own, but for the rebellious acts of many, why is he content or satisfied according to Isaiah 53:11?

9. Do you think this same sentiment of satisfaction or contentment would be shared by Jesus in 1 Peter 3:18? Why or why not?

10. The servant in Isaiah suffered for the sake of others. How does this compare to the attitude of James and John in Mark 10:35-37, Sunday's gospel?

11. What suffering is in store for James and John according to Mark 10:38-40?

12. What does Jesus say is his reason for coming in Mark 10:41-45?

13. What example does Jesus leave us in 1 Peter 2:21?

Reflection

1. Have you ever experienced bullying, or been ridiculed or rejected by your peers? Did you ever ridicule or reject others in your school? Why? Have your children ever been picked on by their peers? How has your attitude changed toward bullying?

2. Were you ever blamed for something you didn't do? How did that make you feel? How would this be a little like Jesus (and the suffering servant) taking the punishment for others? How would it be different?

Twenty-Ninth Sunday of Ordinary Time – Year B

3. This reading from Isaiah is fulfilled by Jesus in the New Testament. Using this Scripture, how would you explain to someone the meaning of Jesus' death and resurrection?

4. This Sunday is Mission Sunday. How can we support the ongoing work of missionaries in the world? How can we be missionaries in the circumstances we are now in?

Optional Exercise before the second reading. Have each person in the group briefly tell something of their past week or of an event anticipated in the coming week. This could be a time to share a triumph, a trial, or a need.

Second Reading — Hebrews 4: 14-16

Setting the Stage

The second reading is from the letter to the Hebrews. It is written about 40 years after the resurrection of Jesus by a Jew who has become a Christian. He is writing to other Hebrews who have become Christians to encourage them in their new-found faith. He does this by showing how everything in the Jewish faith points toward Jesus and is fulfilled in him. Through these words, God our Father is telling us *who our new High Priest is, what he is like and what he means for us.*

Read this reading aloud. Reread this Scripture.
What word, phrase, or idea stands out for you?

Exploring Further

1. What role of Jesus is emphasized in Hebrews 4:14?

2. What is the role of the high priest and where does the priest exercise his priestly function according to Leviticus 16:6, 20-22, 24, 34?

3. What is Jesus' role according to the following?
   Hebrews 2:17
   Hebrews 7:23-25
   Romans 8:34

4. Where does Jesus exercise his priestly function?
   Hebrews 4:14

Come to Me

Hebrews 1:3

Hebrews 8:1

5. Why can we have hope in our profession of faith according to Hebrews 10:23?

6. Why can our high priest relate to us? In what way is he different according to Hebrews 4:15?

7. What did Jesus do for us according to 2 Corinthians 5:21?

8. What can we do without fear? What two things can we receive in Hebrews 4:16?

Reflection

1. How has some difficult life experience helped you to be empathetic, compassionate, or helpful to someone else who was experiencing something similar? Explain.

2. Does the fact that Jesus experienced the weaknesses of humanity and was put the test in every way as we ourselves give you comfort and encouragement? Why or why not?

3. Can you think of a time you turned boldly and confidently to our high priest, Jesus, and received mercy or grace in a time of need? Explain.

4. Our mission is to share our profession of faith in Jesus to the whole world. How can we respect other cultures and still offer Jesus, who gives life and salvation to all? Do you believe this is possible? Why or why not?

Closing Prayer

Lord, have mercy on us as we place our trust in you. Amen.

CHAPTER 8

THIRTIETH SUNDAY OF ORDINARY TIME – YEAR B

OPENING SONG
OPENING PRAYER

Open in prayer and invite everyone to add their own prayer. Close together: "The Lord has done great things for us, and we rejoice.(Psalm 126:3) Amen."

REVIEW STUDY GUIDELINES

First Reading   Jeremiah 31:7-9

Setting the Stage
The first reading is from the book of the prophet Jeremiah. These words were written more than 600 years before Jesus. This part is called the Book of Consolation and through these words God our Father tells the people what he plans for the whole Hebrew nation[7], here called "Jacob." (In the psalm following the reading they are called "Zion.) About 100 years before Jeremiah's time, the Hebrew's northern kingdom, known by two names—Israel and Ephraim—have been conquered, and the people deported to the "land of the north," that is, to Assyria, which is northern Iran and Iraq today. *We hear what God our Father will do for them; it is a sign of his concern for us when we are in distress.*

Read the first reading aloud. Reread this Scripture.
What word, phrase, or idea stands out for you?

Come to Me

Exploring Further

1. Why does God encourage the people to praise in Jeremiah 31:7?

2. What consistent promise is given that these Scriptures are an example of?
    Jeremiah 23:3
    Isaiah 4:4-5
    Isaiah 37:31

3. Where will the people be brought back from according to Jeremiah 31:8a?

4. How are the remnant described?
    Jeremiah 31:8b
    Jeremiah 20:13
    Micah 4:6

5. How is the emotional state of the remnant described in Jeremiah 31:9a?

6. Why might these be tears of repentance?

7. What four images are used to describe how God will lead his people in Jeremiah 31:9?

8. How does God lead and care for his people according to Psalm 23?

9. Jeremiah 31:9 states, "I shall guide them to streams of water." Water is important to the life and religion of the Israelites. What does water symbolize?
    Jeremiah 2:13
    Psalm 36:8-9
    Sirach 15:3
    John 7:37-39

10. How is relationship and affection described in the following?
    Jeremiah 31:9b
    Hosea 11:3-4
    2 Corinthians 6:18

11. How does Jesus restore and in what way does this fulfill the first reading, in Mark 10:46-52, Sunday's gospel?

Thirtieth Sunday of Ordinary Time – Year B

Reflection

1. Can you think of a time you experienced a "scattering" or being separated from family, friends, or church community because of a disagreement or poor choices or life circumstances? How would you describe the "homecoming"?

2. The remnant is described as the weak, wounded, vulnerable, and needy people in society. Why do you think these are the ones named that God gathers in?

3. Where in your life can you relate to or be identified as weak, wounded, vulnerable, or needy? Why is this a good thing?

4. At this time in your life, which of the following do you desire or need? Explain.
    a. Tears of repentance.
    b. Consolation.
    c. To be refreshed by brooks of water (waters of life, wisdom, and the Holy Spirit).
    d. A straight path where you will not stumble.
    e. To know God's love as a father for his first born.
    f. To know God's healing.

Optional Exercise before the second reading. Have each person in the group briefly tell something of their past week or of an event anticipated in the coming week. This could be a time to share a triumph, a trial, or a need.

Second Reading — Hebrews 5:1-6

Setting the Stage

The second reading is from the letter to the Hebrews. It is written about 40 years after the resurrection of Jesus by a Jew who has become a Christian. He is writing to other Hebrews who have become Christians to encourage them in their new-found faith and he does this by drawing on Old Testament texts and customs. Note the names:
1. Aaron: he is the first priest of the Hebrews at the time of Moses, who is his brother.
2. Melchizedek: He is the mysterious king and so-called "eternal" priest who blesses Abraham. (Melchizedek, king of righteousness, priest and king of Salem; blessed Abraham in the name of the Most High God and received tithes from him; type of Christ, the Priest-King.[8])

COME TO ME

Read the second reading aloud. Reread this Scripture.
What word, phrase, or idea stands out for you?

Exploring Further

1. What is the role of the High Priest according to Hebrews 5:1?
   Note: Only the High Priest could enter the Holy of Holies, the presence of God, and he could do so only once a year.[9]

2. How does the sacrifice of the Jewish high priest and the sacrifice of Jesus as high priest, differ according to Hebrews 9:24-28?

3. Why can the high priest relate to the people according to Hebrews 5:2-3?

4. Who is the high priest and what is he commanded to do in Leviticus 9:7?

5. How does one get to be a high priest?
   Hebrews 5:4
   Numbers 16:40 (or Numbers 17:5)

6. How is Christ appointed High Priest?
   Hebrews 5:5-6
   John 8:54

Reflection

1. In your work, church community, community activities, or home, or other positions in life, how have you been called forth, appointed, or chosen? How did God supply what you needed to do the job?

2. Hebrews 5:2-3 suggests the priest should be gentle with the wayward and ignorant because he has the same weaknesses that also need a sin offering. Have you experienced people in authority who deal gently and wisely with others? Explain.

3. Does awareness of your own weaknesses help you deal gently with others' weaknesses or are you critical and sharp with people who have similar weaknesses as you? Explain.

Closing Prayer

We give thanks that we all have access to God through our High Priest, Jesus Christ, who gave himself up as a fragrant offering for us. Amen.

CHAPTER 9
THIRTY-FIRST SUNDAY OF ORDINARY TIME – YEAR B

OPENING SONG
OPENING PRAYER

Open in prayer and invite everyone to add their own prayer. Close together: "You, O God, are our rock, our refuge, our shield and our salvation. The Lord is our God, the Lord alone. Amen."

REVIEW STUDY GUIDELINES

First Reading   Deuteronomy 6:2-6

Setting the Stage

The first reading is from the book of the Deuteronomy. We find Moses, in 1300 BC, speaking to the Hebrew people just before they enter the Promised Land of Palestine; it is called "the land of milk and honey." The last four lines of this reading give us the famous Jewish daily prayer called the "Shema," which means "hear." Through this prayer *God our Father wants us to hear what the most important thing in our lives is.*

Read the first reading aloud. Reread this Scripture.
What word, phrase, or idea stands out for you?

COME TO ME

Exploring Further

1. What instructions does Moses give the people before they enter the Promised Land and what are the two blessings for obedience mentioned in Deuteronomy 6:1-3?

2. Moses prays that the Israelites will "fear the Lord all their days." What do the following Scriptures indicate "fear of the Lord" means?
   Genesis 22:12
   Joshua 24:14
   Proverbs 1:7
   Jeremiah 32:39-40

3. What is the result of obedience in the following Scriptures?
   Exodus 15:26
   Deuteronomy 30:15-16, 19-20
   Luke 11:28

4. How does Moses express the core of the law in Deuteronomy 6:4-5?

5. How is the core of our faith summarized in Mark 12:28-32, Sunday's gospel?

6. What does God ask of his people in Deuteronomy 10:12-13?

7. What priority should be given to these commands according to Deuteronomy 6:6-9?

8. How will God help us remember these commands in Jeremiah 31:31-33?

Reflection

1. Do you see obedience as a blessing for good and a means to freedom or do you see obedience as a prohibition and taking away of freedom? Explain. What is Scripture's perspective on obedience?

2. In the above Scriptures fear of God: is demonstrated by obedience; means to serve in faithfulness and throw out all false gods; is the beginning of wisdom; and is for our own good. Can you relate to this understanding of "fear of God"? Explain. What definition would you give "fear of God"? How have you experienced the "fear of God"?

3. Regarding God's laws, the Israelites were exhorted to take them to heart, drill them into their children, speak them at work and at rest, bind them to your wrist and foreheads, and write them on your doors. God said he will put his laws in our minds and write them on our hearts. What are

Thirty-First Sunday of Ordinary Time – Year B

some ways, individually and as a community, we take to heart and integrate God's teachings in our day-to-day lives?

4. The core of our faith is to love God with all our heart, mind, and strength and to love our neighbor as ourself. This command requires an attitude of the heart that flows forth in action. How can you enter into and live out this command as a way of life?

Optional Exercise before the second reading. Have each person in the group briefly tell something of their past week or of an event anticipated in the coming week. This could be a time to share a triumph, a trial, or a need.

Second Reading   Hebrews 7:23-28

Setting the Stage

The second reading is from the letter to the Hebrews. It is written about 40 years after the resurrection of Jesus by a Jew who has become a Christian. He is writing to other Hebrews who have become Christians to encourage them in their new-found faith. He does this by pointing out that the New Testament times of Jesus fulfill and explain the texts and customs of the Jewish Law which is known by these names—the Old Testament, the old covenant, and the first covenant. God our Father here describes *who Jesus is for us*.

Read the second reading aloud. Reread this Scripture.
What word, phrase, or idea stands out for you?

Exploring Further

1. How does Jesus' priesthood differ from the old covenant priesthood in Hebrews 7:23-24?

2. As high priest, what does Jesus continually do?
   Hebrews 7:25
   Romans 8:31-34

3. What characterizes Jesus our high priest in Hebrews 7:26?

4. What tribe or order do the priests of the Old Covenant belong to in Numbers 18:2, 6-7?

Come to Me

5. What order does the priest Melchizedek belong to in Genesis 14:18-19?

6. What order of priesthood does Jesus belong to and why?
   Psalm 110:4
   Hebrews 7:11-17

7. What is the difference in the old covenant sacrifice offered by the priests and the sacrifice offered by our high priest Jesus?
   Hebrews 7:27-28
   Hebrews 9:25-28
   Hebrews 10:11-14

8. What is better than sacrifice according to Mark 12:32-33, Sunday's gospel?

9. How does Jesus respond to the scribe's insight in Mark 12:34?

Reflection

1. Only Jesus, the perfect sacrifice and perfect high priest, can sanctify us and lead us to the Father. Just as the priests from the tribe of Levi cannot effectively sanctify the people, our own sacrifices and good works can not save us. Have you ever tried to earn your own salvation? Explain. How do you receive and live the new covenant life Jesus brought about?

2. Jesus suffered, died, and rose again—once for all sin. In the Eucharist, Jesus' passion, death, and resurrection is made present, not repeated. When you repent, Jesus forgives; all sin, past, present, and future was atoned for at the crucifixion and does not add to Jesus' suffering now. When you suffer, are abused, neglected, and so on, Jesus shares in your suffering. His passion is made present; not repeated. "Where time and space in some way 'merge' and the drama of Golgotha is re-presented in a living way..." (Pope John Paul II, *On the Eucharist* #59). Does anything hold you back from taking your sin or suffering to Jesus? Explain. How have you experienced the presence of Jesus during times of suffering?

3. Jesus our high priest is constantly interceding for us. What image does this bring to your mind? For what situation does this give you hope?

Closing Prayer

Lord, we desire to serve you with all our heart, mind, and strength. Lead us to life. Amen.

CHAPTER 10

ALL SAINTS
ONLY WHEN SUNDAY FALLS ON NOVEMBER 1ST

OPENING SONG
OPENING PRAYER

Open in prayer and invite everyone to add their own prayer. Close together: "Lord, we give to you praise and glory and wisdom, thanksgiving and honor and power and strength to our God for ever and ever. Amen."

REVIEW STUDY GUIDELINES

First Reading   Revelation 7:2-4, 9-14

Setting the Stage

The first reading is from the book of Revelation. It is written by a Christian named John about 100 AD and is meant to encourage Christians to persevere in their faith as they face persecution and trials.[10] It is an inspired picture-book appealing to our imagination. The pictures are not to be interpreted literally; they are intended to create a total impression of eternal realities.[11] The book of Revelation is an "epic of Christian hope", the victory song of the church.[12] The symbols in this reading are:

1. The number 144, 000: this is a multiple of 12; "12" in the Bible is a symbol of completeness. "144, 000" means the immense crowd of all those who have been faithful; not one is missing in heaven.[13]
2. A "seal [or mark] on the forehead:" like a badge, a seal is a symbol of belonging to God.[14]
3. Palm branches: a palm branch is a symbol of victory.
4. "The Elders" are angels in heaven, and symbols of the 12 patriarchs and 12 apostles.[15]

COME TO ME

5. "The four Living Creatures:" are four angels directing the universe.[16]

We hear the answer to the question: *Will wrongs ever be righted?*

Read the first reading aloud. Reread this Scripture.
What word, phrase, or idea stands out for you?

Exploring Further

1. Where are the angels stationed in Revelation 7:1?

2. Why is this significant?
   Jeremiah 49:36, 39
   Ezekiel 7:2-4
   Matthew 24:30-31

3. What holds back the four winds of judgment and what do the elect receive in Revelation 7:2-3?

4. What sign or seal is given in the following and why?
   Exodus 12:7, 12-14
   Ezekiel 9:3-6
   2 Corinthians 1:21-22
   Ephesians 1:7, 13-14

5. Who receives the seal and what does this number mean according to "Setting the Stage" and to Revelation 7:4?

6. How does this fulfill the promise made to Abraham in Genesis 15:5?

7. What does John see in Revelation 7:9-12? Where are these people from? What is everyone doing? What do the palm branches symbolize?

8. Who are these people according to the following?
   Revelation 7:13-15
   Revelation 15:2-3
   Daniel 12:1-3

9. How are the saints purified according to Revelation 7:14?

10. What is the reward to the faithful according to Revelation 7:16-17?

11. What does Jesus promise to the faithful in Mathew 5:1-12, Sunday's gospel?

All Saints (Only When Sunday Falls on November 1st)

Reflection

1. It is clear that those who receive salvation will be from every nation, every tongue, and every tribe. This means not everyone will be from your denomination or even from a Christian denomination. How might this larger perspective of heaven cause you to question some "pat" answers about salvation you may hold? In what ways do Christians sometimes put their idea of God and heaven in a box?

2. Those who receive the seal are faithful, wise and righteous; grieve and lament detestable things done; hear the gospel and receive it. They have made a firm decision for Jesus, followed by action. Jesus said those who live vulnerable lives trusting God, who are humble, who hunger and thirst for righteousness, are merciful, pure of heart, peacemakers, and who stand firm when persecuted for righteousness will be rewarded. What firm decision and action do you need to make? How can you grow in these attitudes in your life so God can transform you into the type of person described in the beatitudes regardless of the cost? Explain.

3. On All Saints Day we remember the communion of saints, those who have been faithful and now enjoy the reward of God who is eternally sheltering, caring for, and comforting them. What "saint" is an example and encouragement to you?

Optional Exercise before the second reading. Have each person in the group briefly tell something of their past week or of an event anticipated in the coming week. This could be a time to share a triumph, a trial, or a need.

Second Reading   1 John 3:1-3

Setting the Stage

The next reading is from the first letter of John. It is written around 90 AD to the Christians who are close to St. John the Apostle. The problem is they are divided over their beliefs. On this feast of All Saints, God our Father teaches us *who we are as human beings, and what we, with the saints, can expect after this life.*

Read the second reading aloud. Reread this Scripture.
What word, phrase, or idea stands out for you?

Come to Me

Exploring Further

1. According to the following, how has God shown his love for us?
   1 John 3:1
   Romans 8:35-39

2. Who can become God's children according to John 1:12?

3. How will the world treat God's children and why? (See definition of "world" in appendix two.)
   Matthew 5:11-12, Sunday's gospel
   John 15:20-21
   John 16:2-3

4. We are God's children now. What will we become?
   1 John 3:2
   1 Corinthians 13:12
   Philippians 3:20-21
   Colossians 3:4

5. If we value his promise, how will we act?
   1 John 3:3
   Hebrews 12:1-2
   Matthew 5:48-6:6

Reflection

1. Today on All Saints Day we celebrate God's children who received Jesus, believed in his name, and stood firm to the end. Can you think of how some of these saints were received and treated in this world? How are you treated in this world because of your faith?

2. The following is a description of what God's children will become according to the Scriptures read today. We do not know; we will be like him; we will be citizens in heaven; our bodies will be transformed to be as his glorious body; we will appear with him in glory; we see poorly now as in a mirror, then we will see face to face and know fully and be fully known. What does this description suggest to you? Does it give you hope? Why or why not?

3. Until Jesus comes again, we are called to purify ourselves and pray and do well, not for show but for God. What are practical ways we can seek to live this way?

All Saints (Only When Sunday Falls on November 1st)

Closing Prayer

Lord, we thank you for the saints and their witness to us. Since we are surrounded by so great a cloud of witnesses, let us also lay aside every weight and the sin that clings so closely, and let us run with perseverance the race that is set before us, looking to Jesus the pioneer and perfecter of our faith. Amen (Hebrews 12:1-2).

CHAPTER 11

ALL SOULS YEAR B
ONLY WHEN SUNDAY FALLS ON NOVEMBER 2ND

OPENING SONG
OPENING PRAYER

Open in prayer and invite everyone to add their own prayer. Close together: "Give those who have died eternal rest, O Lord, and may your light shine on them forever. Amen."

REVIEW STUDY GUIDELINES

Note: The liturgical context of these readings on All Souls Day is that of praying for the dead, who are not yet in heaven. "All who have died in God's grace and friendship, but still imperfectly purified, are indeed assured of their eternal salvation; but after death they undergo purification, so as to achieve the holiness necessary to enter the joy of heaven."[17] Instead of assuming those who have died are already in heaven, the church prays for them.

First Reading   Isaiah 25:6-9

Setting the Stage

The first reading is from a special part of the book of the prophet Isaiah called the "Apocalypse of Isaiah." We hear of a vision of heaven, a promise of *what God our Father has in store for our loved ones who have died*. Note the phrase "On this mountain." This refers to Mount Zion, the hill on which Jerusalem is built; it became a symbol of heaven, but also it has become a symbol of us, the church.

Come to Me

Read the first reading aloud. Reread this Scripture. What word, phrase, or idea stands out for you?

Exploring Further

1. What will be provided in the heavenly Jerusalem and for whom, according to Isaiah 25:6?

2. What does Jesus say about this Messianic banquet in Luke 14:13-14, 16-24?

3. How does Jesus feed us now according to John 6:51, 54?

4. What will God do for us in the heavenly Jerusalem according to Isaiah 25:7-8?

5. What do the following Scriptures say regarding death, suffering, and pain?
   1 Corinthians 15:26
   Revelation 21:4

6. How will the people respond in the heavenly Jerusalem according to Isaiah 25:9?

7. Who is Jesus identified as in Mark 8:27-29, Sunday's gospel?

8. What price is paid to provide the Messianic banquet according to Mark 8:31-33?

9. How will we share in the Messianic banquet?

10. What is done for the soldiers who died fighting for God and why in 2 Maccabees 12:38-46? (See appendix one.)

11. What does 1 Corinthians 2:10-15 tell us about the purifying of our lives?

Reflection

1. What loved ones in your life have gone on ahead and you can remember and pray for especially on All Souls Day? Do you find it comforting to know that when you die the church will pray for you, too? Why or why not?

2. In the parable about the Messianic banquet in Luke, many were invited to the banquet and chose not to come. In John's gospel we are told the food and wine we are provided with is the body and blood of Jesus. How might choosing not to regularly receive the Eucharist banquet be similar to

All Souls Year B (Only When Sunday Falls on November 2nd)

choosing not to attend the Messianic banquet? Is it possible that if we choose not to receive the Eucharistic banquet we may end up choosing to not attend the heavenly banquet? Why do you think so?

3. Jesus said the cost of following after him is surrendering or not clinging to our lives. This pattern of dying to sin and rising to life began with baptism and is to be continued throughout life. What do you think a surrendered life looks like?
What have you had to surrender (large or small) and what life, freedom, or growth resulted from this surrendering or dying to your will?

4. God's grace and mercy is available now. What can you do to be purified from sin and attachments in this life rather than after death? Are the lives of the saints an example and encouragement to you that this is possible? Why or why not?

Optional Exercise before the second reading. Have each person in the group briefly tell something of their past week or of an event anticipated in the coming week. This could be a time to share a triumph, a trial, or a need.

Second Reading   1 Corinthians 15:12-26

Setting the Stage

The next reading is from the first letter of St. Paul written to the church in Corinth, Greece, about the year 55 AD. "Greeks have no trouble in conceiving the immortality of the soul, but the idea of a raised body is difficult."[18] To them the human body has no value after death. Paul makes a comparison between Adam and the Lord Jesus Christ. Through these words, God our Father shows us *why we believe that our bodies will rise and what will happen at the end of time.*

Read the second reading aloud. Reread this Scripture.
What word, phrase, or idea stands out for you?

Exploring Further

1. What is the issue of contention in 1 Corinthians 15:12?

2. What would no resurrection mean to our Christian faith according to
   1 Corinthians 15:13-14, 17-19?

3. What was the role of the apostles?
   1 Corinthians 15:15
   Acts 1:21-22
   Acts 22:14-15

4. How does death enter the world and what is God's answer?
   1 Corinthians 15:20-23
   Romans 6:23?

5. What is God's plan to bring life according to John 1:1-5, 9-14, Sunday's alternate gospel?

6. What is the result in believing in the resurrection?
   John 11:25
   Romans 10:9

7. What does Jesus' resurrection mean to each of us?
   Romans 8:11
   1 Thessalonians 4:14

8. What will happen in the end according to the following?
   1 Corinthians 15:24-26
   1 Thessalonians 4:16-17
   Revelation 20:12-15
   Revelation 21:3-4

Reflection

1. What questions arise in your mind when you think of death and dying?

2. In the funeral liturgy we say that life is changed not ended. "Therefore our union with the brethren who have gone to sleep in the peace of Christ is not in the least weakened or interrupted, but on the contrary, according to the perpetual faith of the Church, is strengthened by the communication of spiritual goods."[19] Have you experienced a continued union with loved ones who have died? Explain.

3. *"What is* "rising"? In death, the separation of the soul from the body, the human body decays and the soul goes to meet God, while awaiting its reunion with its glorified body. God, in his almighty

All Souls Year B (Only When Sunday Falls on November 2nd)

power, will definitively grant incorruptible life to our bodies by reuniting them with our souls through the power of Jesus' resurrection. *Who will rise?* All the dead will rise, "those who have done well, to the resurrection of life, and those who have done evil, to the resurrection of judgment." How? Christ is raised with his own body. So, in him, "all of them will rise again with their own bodies which they now bear," but Christ "will change our lowly body to be like his glorious body, into a spiritual body."[20] In the early church there was much controversy over the resurrection of the body. Some the early Christians gave their lives defending this doctrine and many turned away because they could not accept this teaching. Is this belief of our faith hard for you or comforting? Explain.

Closing Prayer

Give our departed brothers and sisters eternal rest, O Lord, for you are rich in mercy. Amen.

CHAPTER 12

DEDICATION OF ST. JOHN LATERAN
ONLY WHEN SUNDAY FALLS ON NOVEMBER 9TH

OPENING SONG
OPENING PRAYER

Open in prayer and invite everyone to add their own prayer. Close together: "Lord, we desire that from our hearts flow streams of living water out to a thirsty people. Amen."

REVIEW STUDY GUIDELINES

First Reading   Ezekiel 47:1-2, 8-9, 12

Setting the Stage

The first reading is from the book of the prophet Ezekiel. These words are inspired by Ezekiel and written by his followers as the Jewish community struggled to keep their Jewish faith while in exile in Babylon, which is in Iraq today, in the 6th century BC. Note the name *Arabah*—it is the name of the dry valley south of the Dead Sea.[21] This is an appropriate reading as we celebrate the dedication of a special church, a special "temple," called the Cathedral Church of the Popes. We hear of a vision showing the *importance of God our Father's presence in the temple* in Jerusalem, and what good effects would flow from him to his people who are faithful.

Read the first reading aloud. Reread this Scripture.
What word, phrase, or idea stands out for you?

Come to Me

Exploring Further

1. What is Ezekiel shown in Ezekiel 47:1-2?

2. The sea of salt water referred to in Ezekiel 47:8 is the Dead Sea where nothing can live, yet what is promised in Ezekiel 47:9?

3. What results from the water flowing from the temple according to Ezekiel 47:7-8, 12?

4. What does water symbolize in the following Scriptures?
   Ezekiel 19:10
   Jeremiah 17:7-8
   Zechariah 13:1

5. What connection does this river of life have to Genesis 2:8-10?

6. The river in Ezekiel is similar to the river mentioned in Revelation 22:1-3. What does the river symbolize?

7. How does Jesus refer to himself in John 2:19-22, Sunday's gospel?

8. What flows from this temple in John 19:34?
   On the Feast of Tabernacles, thousands of Jews would go to Jerusalem to celebrate the feast, remembering the time when Moses brought water from a rock. They thanked God for providing water in the past year and prayed that He would do the same in the coming year. They looked forward to a time when water would pour out of the temple, as prophesied by Ezekiel, becoming deeper and deeper and bringing life, fruitfulness, and healing wherever it went. This passage in Ezekiel 47 was read at the Feast of Tabernacles and enacted visually. The high priest would go down to the pool of Siloam and fill a golden pitcher with water. He would then lead the people to the temple, where he would pour water through a funnel in the west side of the altar, and into the ground, in anticipation of the great river that would flow from the temple. According to Rabbinic tradition, Jerusalem was the navel of the earth and the temple of Mount Zion was the center of the navel (its "belly" or "innermost being").[22]

9. On the last day of the Feast of Tabernacles, what did Jesus stand up and proclaim in John 7:37-38? (Note: "heart" could be translated "innermost being.")

10. What is the result to those who believe in Jesus?
    John 7:38
    John 4:13-14

11. How are the people of God described in 1 Corinthians 3:16-17?

Dedication of St. John of Lateran (Only When Sunday Falls on November 9th)

This is amazing! Ezekiel prophesies that water will flow from the temple bringing life. Jesus says he is the temple that provides living water. All who believe are the temple of God. Living water flows from the temple (believers in Jesus) and fulfills the prophesy in Ezekiel.

Reflection

1. The water flowing from Jesus (his Spirit) brings life, healing, and abundance—so much so that places of death can be transformed into places of life. Are you parched and thirsty, sipping occasionally, wading cautiously, or immersing yourself in the living water? Explain.

2. Where has this life of Jesus, flowing through the church and/or believers (the community) nourished you, or brought life or healing?

3. The living water of Jesus flows through the heart of the believer. The catechism of the Catholic Church says; "the heart is the dwelling-place where I am, where I live; the heart is our hidden centre. The heart is the place of decision, the place of truth, where we choose life or death. It is the place of encounter; it is the place of covenant."[23]
What picture or image does this bring to your mind?

4. St. Theresa of Avalon reflects on the relationship of spiritual growth and self-knowledge. Has your spiritual growth paralleled your awareness of self and growth? Explain.

Optional Exercise before the second reading. Have each person in the group briefly tell something of their past week or of an event anticipated in the coming week. This could be a time to share a triumph, a trial, or a need.

Second Reading   1 Corinthians 3:9-11, 16-17

Setting the Stage

The next reading is from the first letter St. Paul wrote to the church in Corinth, Greece, about 25 years after the resurrection of Jesus. He had received reports that there were divisions in the Corinthian church over the question of which of their priests they would follow. In response, Paul compares a church to a building. Through these words *God our Father tells us who is its foundation, the One who keeps everyone together.* These are appropriate words as we celebrate the famous building called St. John Lateran.

Read the second reading aloud. Reread this Scripture.
What word, phrase, or idea stands out for you?

Come to Me

Exploring Further

1. What does Paul compare the Corinthians (and us) to in 1 Corinthians 3:9?

2. How does Paul describe his work and how does he build in 1 Corinthians 3:10-11?

3. How are believers described?
   Ephesians 2:19-20
   1 Peter 2:4-5?

4. What does Paul want clearly understood and what makes the Christian community a fit abode for God in 1 Corinthians 3:16?

5. What does Paul say to preachers and teachers who destroy rather than build in 1 Corinthians 3:17?

6. How does Paul describe the spiritual work of leaders and teachers in the church and who ultimately will judge their work according to 1 Corinthians 3:10b-15?

7. What happens in the temple and how did Jesus react in John 2:13-16, Sunday's gospel?

8. What do the following Scriptures say about the temple?
   2 Corinthians 6:16
   Revelation 21:22

Reflection

1. The church is both visible and spiritual. We need visible reminders of invisible truths. St. John Lateran is a visible church that reminds us that Jesus entrusted the visible church to be the keeper of faith, and to speak and pass on truth in His name. What does this say of the important teaching role of the church? What responsibility does this give teachers and leaders in building and cultivating in the lives of each generation?

2. What might happen when we think of the temple or church in terms of a building only? Do you see the people of God being the dwelling place or temple, and the church being the body of Christ and the spotless spouse? How do these images change or expand your understanding of church?

3. When you consider yourself a living stone in the temple of the living God, what does this say to you regarding your value? What does it say to you about the value of those you worship with each week?

Closing Prayer

Lord, we desire to be like living stones built on Christ as a spiritual house, a holy people. Amen.

CHAPTER 13

Thirty-Second Sunday of Ordinary Time – Year B

Opening Song
Opening Prayer

Open in prayer and invite everyone to add their own prayer. Close together: "God of power and mercy, protect us from all harm. It is the Lord who lifts up those who are bowed down, loves the righteous, watches over the stranger, and upholds the orphan and widow. Amen."

Review Study Guidelines

First Reading   1 Kings 17:10-16

Setting the Stage

This reading is from the first book of Kings. We hear of an event in the life of the great prophet Elijah who lived 850 years before Jesus. We find him in the town of Zarephath, or Sarepta, located in what is southern Lebanon today; it is during the time of a long drought. Note the word "meal"—it is a type of flour used for baking. God our Father gives us an example of *what happens when a person is generous.*

Read the first reading aloud. Reread this Scripture.
What word, phrase, or idea stands out for you?

Come to Me

Exploring Further

1. At the time of this reading, the king of Israel is Ahab. What do we discover in 1 Kings 16:30-33 about Ahab and who Ahab worshipped?

2. Those who worship Baal believed he is the god who brought the rains and bountiful harvests.[24] What does Elijah prophesy to Ahab and what does this imply about the power of Baal and the power of the God of Israel in 1 Kings 17:1?

3. After making this prophesy, what must Elijah do, and how does God look after him in 1 Kings 17:2-6?

4. After the water dries up, where does God tell Elijah to go and who will provide for him there according to 1 Kings 17:7-9?

5. When Elijah sees the widow, what does he ask her for in 1 Kings 17:10-11?

6. What is the widow's situation in 1 Kings 17:12?

7. What promise does Elijah make in 1 Kings 17:13-14?

8. What choice does the widow make and what is the result in 1 Kings 17:15-16?

9. In the time of Elijah the famine caused the widow hardship. What is the hardship to widows that Jesus mentions in Mark 12:38-40?

10. How does the widow's action in Elijah's time compare with the widow in Mark 12:41-44, Sunday's gospel?

Reflection

1. God used ravens (which were considered unclean) and a foreign widow to provide for Elijah. What does this say to you about how God sees people and things as compared to how we often see people and things?

2. In a drought in your life—a material or financial drought, a relationship drought, a spiritual drought, or an emotional drought—when you felt hopeless, depressed, angry, and so forth, how did God provide for you in strange and unexpected ways?

3. The widow, in obedience, gave from her poverty and God faithfully supplied her needs. When in your life did you obediently give of your time (though you were busy), of your resources (though you could barely make ends meet), of your faith by praying with someone or sharing hope in Jesus

Thirty-Second Sunday of Ordinary Time – Year B

(though you felt inadequate and uncomfortable), in other ways (where you felt unequal to the task) and afterward realized that God provided when you stepped out in faith?

Optional Exercise before the second reading. Have each person in the group briefly tell something of their past week or of an event anticipated in the coming week. This could be a time to share a triumph, a trial, or a need.

Second Reading   Hebrews 9: 24-28

Setting the Stage

The second reading is from the letter to the Hebrews written about 40 years after the resurrection of Jesus by a Jew who had become a Christian. He's encouraging other Jews who had become Christians to persevere in their new-found faith by showing that everything in the Jewish faith pointed to Jesus. In this reading he makes a comparison of the role of the Jewish High Priest with what Jesus did. Through these words *God our Father tells us what Jesus does for us "at the end of the age," that is at the appointed time.*

Read the second reading aloud. Reread this Scripture.
What word, phrase, or idea stands out for you?

Exploring Further

1. Where does Jesus enter after the resurrection? Who does Jesus appear before? And on whose behalf is Jesus appearing according to Hebrews 9:24?

2. What do the priests in the Old Testament do and what does this prefigure in Hebrews 9:6-7, 25?

3. What long awaited event is the culmination of salvation history and termed the "fullness of time" or "end of the age" that is referred to in Hebrews 9:26?

4. How does John the Baptist announce this moment in history in John 1:29-34?

5. What follows the death of humans according to Hebrews 9:27?

6. What do we eagerly await and why in Hebrews 9:28?

7. What do you learn about the second coming from the following?

Come to Me

Acts 3:19-21
Philippians 3:20-21

Reflection

1. God's plan for the world has been unfolding since the beginning of time, to the coming of Jesus, to the waiting for the second and final coming of Jesus. Would you prefer Jesus returned soon or not for a much longer time? Why?

2. Why do you think the author of Hebrews explained in such detail the role of the priests and high priest, the role of blood sacrifices and intercession, and connected this with the role of Jesus? What does this say to you about God's plans and attention to detail?

3. After death comes judgment (verse 27). Christ has dealt with sin and will return to bring salvation to those who are waiting for him (verse 28). Considering these two truths, how do you plan to prepare and wait?

Closing Prayer

Lord, pour out your Spirit upon us and keep us single-minded in your service. Amen.

CHAPTER 14
Thirty-Third Sunday of Ordinary Time – Year B

Opening Song
Opening Prayer

Open in prayer and invite everyone to add their own prayer. Close together: "Keep me safe, O God; you are my hope. You show me the path of life and in your presence is the fullness of joy. Amen."

Review Study Guidelines

First Reading — Daniel 12:1-3

Setting the Stage

The first reading is from the book of Daniel written to encourage the Hebrew people suffering during the Greek persecution in the second century BC. This reading is a magnificent poetic conclusion to the vision of an angel speaking to the Jewish boy, Daniel, the hero of this book. There is mention of a certain "Michael." This is the patron angel of the Hebrew people. Through these words *God our Father tells us who is in charge of history and what his people can expect in the future.*

Read the first reading aloud. Reread this Scripture.
What word, phrase, or idea stands out for you?

Come to Me

Exploring Further

1. How is the angel Michael described in Daniel 12:1a?

2. What information is given about Michael in the following Scriptures?
   Daniel 10:13, 21
   Jude: 9
   Revelation 12:7-8

3. What is to come and who will be spared in Daniel 12:1b?

4. What does Jesus say about this time in Mark 13:24-27, Sunday's gospel?

5. What do the following Scriptures say about the Book of Life?
   Exodus 32:32-33
   Psalm 139:15 (or verse 16)
   Luke 10:20
   Revelation 20:12

6. What will happen according to Daniel 12:2?

7. What further information about the resurrection of the body is given?
   2 Maccabees 7: 9-14 (See appendix one.)
   Isaiah 66:22-24
   Matthew 22:30-32
   John 5:28-29

8. How are the wise and the righteous described in the following Scriptures?
   Daniel 12:3
   Matthew 13:43
   1 Corinthians 15:41-44

Reflection

1. Michael is described as an archangel, protector of the people and prince. Have you ever experienced the presence or protection of angels? Explain.

2. "Serious reflection on the Lord's second coming is the first step to overcoming our anxieties about what the future holds for us. We come to the realization that each of us holds the key to our own future in heaven through the way we spend our lives on earth."[25] In the light of the Scriptures in

Thirty-Third Sunday of Ordinary Time – Year B

this study, what in your life now are good choices you will continue? What in your life will you choose to change? How can you have your name written in the Book of Life?

3. How can we be stars in God's sight? Who do you know that is a star shining for God?

Optional Exercise before the second reading. Have each person in the group briefly tell something of their past week or of an event anticipated in the coming week. This could be a time to share a triumph, a trial, or a need.

Second Reading   Hebrews 10:11-14

Setting the Stage

The second reading is from the letter to the Hebrews written about 40 years after the resurrection of Jesus by a Jew who had become a Christian. He's writing to other Hebrews who had become Christians to encourage them in their new-found faith. He does this by showing how everything in the Jewish faith and all that the Jewish priest would do, pointed toward Jesus, and is fulfilled in him. He gives a quote from the famous Psalm 110 which speaks of the Priest Messiah. *God our Father is telling us what that Messiah, who is His Son, Jesus, has done for us.*

Read the second reading aloud. Reread this Scripture.
What word, phrase, or idea stands out for you?

Exploring Further

1. Why is the work of the priests never done according to Hebrews 10:11?

2. What does "Jesus sat down at the right hand of God" mean in Hebrews 10:12?

3. What further understanding of this statement is found in Acts 2:32-36?

4. What does Christ's offering do for us according to the following Scriptures?
   Hebrews 10:14
   John 17:19
   Note: We have been made perfect (complete in Christ), yet we are being made holy (sanctified). Through his death and resurrection, Christ made his believers perfect in God's sight. At the same

time, he is making them holy (progressively cleansed and set apart for God's special use) in their daily pilgrimage here.[26]

5. What does this sacrifice call us to according to Colossians 3:1-4?

6. Why is there no longer a need for a sin offering according to Hebrews 10:17-18?

Reflection

1. We are complete and perfect in Christ and at the same time in the process of being sanctified or made holy. What does this mean to you? Is this encouraging, surprising, shocking, shameful, or hopeful for you? Explain.

2. Where in your life can you see progress has been made in this process of holiness?

3. Where in your life today is God calling you to greater holiness?

Closing Prayer

For me it is good to be near God; I have made the Lord God my refuge. Amen (Psalm 73:28).

CHAPTER 15

CHRIST THE KING YEAR B

OPENING SONG
OPENING PRAYER

Open in prayer and invite everyone to add their own prayer. Close together: "Christ our King may all heaven and earth acclaim your glory and never cease to praise you. Amen."

REVIEW STUDY GUIDELINES

First Reading   Daniel 7:13-14

Setting the Stage

The first reading is from the book of the prophet Daniel written about 165 BC to encourage the Hebrew people who are persecuted by the Greek Empire. In this reading the hero of the book, Daniel, is describing a vision. These are appropriate words as we celebrate this feast of Christ the King because they paint a picture of a coronation ceremony. The "Ancient One" is God our Father, the Master and Lord of history, who, through these words, is telling us *who his Son Jesus really is.* [Christ the King Sunday marks the end of the church year.]

Read the first reading aloud. Reread this Scripture.
What word, phrase, or idea stands out for you?

COME TO ME

Exploring Further

1. What does Daniel see in his vision in Daniel 7:13?

2. How does Jesus refer to himself in Matthew 8:20?

3. What significance do "clouds" have?
   Exodus 16:10
   Exodus 19:9

4. What is taking place in Daniel 7:14a?

5. Who are the subjects of this kingdom and for how long according to Daniel 7:14b?

6. How does Daniel's vision compare with Revelation 14:14?

7. What two responses would be appropriate when contemplating Christ the King and the kingdom that he has established?
   Matthew 4:17
   Hebrews 12:28

8. What does Jesus say about himself and his kingdom in John 18:33-38, Sunday's gospel?

Reflection

1. What thoughts or reactions do you have when you picture or contemplate Christ the King coming in glory and crowned with everlasting kingship?

2. What allegiance, in times past, did subjects have for the king? In what ways should our allegiance to Christ the King be similar? How does it differ?

Optional Exercise before the second reading. Have each person in the group briefly tell something of their past week or of an event anticipated in the coming week. This could be a time to share a triumph, a trial, or a need.

Christ the King Year B

Second Reading   Revelation 1:5-8

Setting the Stage

The second reading is from the book of Revelation written during the persecution of Christians by the Roman Empire about 100 AD. It is important to know that the international language of the time, and the language of the New Testament, was Greek. We hear now two letters of that Greek alphabet: ALPHA, symbolizing the One by whom all things are created, and OMEGA, which means the One to whom all things are directed. *This Lord of history, God our Father, tells us what position he has given to his Son, Jesus.* Note the expression, "tribes of the earth will lament." These are the people who rejected Jesus and who will live to regret that decision.

Read the second reading aloud. Reread this Scripture.
What word, phrase, or idea stands out for you?

Exploring Further

1. In what three ways is Jesus described in Revelation 1:5a?

2. What is the promise made to David as stated in Isaiah 55:3-5?

3. What is God's answer to all His promises according to 2 Corinthians 1:20?

4. As the ruler of kings, what area does Jesus claim kingship of in John 18:36-38, Sunday's gospel?

5. What statements regarding truth does Jesus make?
   John 8:31-32
   John 14:6

6. What does Jesus do for us and how according to Revelation 1:5b?

7. For those who turn to the Messiah to receive forgiveness through his blood, what does Jesus make us and with what results according to Revelation 1:6?

8. Who are we in Christ and what does it call us to according to 1 Peter 2:9?

9. How is the coming of our King described and who will witness this event in Revelation 1:7a?

10. What will the people who rejected Jesus do according to 'Setting the Stage' notes and Revelation 1:7b?

11. What do the following Scriptures say regarding the kingship of Jesus over all creation?
    Revelation 1:8
    Isaiah 48:12-13
    Zechariah 12:1-2, 10

Reflection

CHRIST THE KING[27] Christ is king in three ways:

- He is the one through whom the whole created universe has been made. Throughout the Word of God all things were made. Without him nothing comes into existence nor remains in existence. He holds the whole universe in his hand. We have nothing to fear, then, from any creature. They can act only if, and so far as, he permits.
- He is King of hearts. All that is fine, lovely and attractive in creatures is so only through sharing in his beauty and goodness. What we seek in reaching out to things is found in the highest degree in him. In him our restless heart finds repose. All our desires are satisfied.
- He is Truth and the final answer to all our questions. Our mind, which longs to understand, finds the truth in him. We learn in knowing him where things have come from, why they exist, and what their destiny is. We learn the highest and profoundest truths about ourselves too, who we are, why we are here and what is the meaning of all we do, and we learn of the goal towards which we tend. *Christ is King of the universe, of our hearts, and of our minds.*

1. *Jesus: King of Creation*
   He holds all creation in his hands. We have nothing to fear. Does this give you hope? Why or why not? At this point in your life, are you able to trust the King of creation in all circumstances and not be afraid? Explain.

2. *Jesus: King of Our Hearts*
   Have you tried to find peace and fulfillment in worldly pursuits or in self-fulfillment? What was the result? Have you given Jesus kingship over your heart? What was the result?

3. *Jesus: King of Our Minds*
   Pilate asked, "What is truth?" How would you answer this question? How do you seek and recognize truth? Can all knowledge and information be looked at in light of what God has revealed? Why or why not? Have you chosen to surrender your mind to the Lordship of Jesus? Explain.

Closing Prayer

Christ, king of all creation, bring us to the joy of your kingdom. Amen.

SECTION TWO

ADVENT

The word Advent means "to come."

The first Sunday of Advent begins the new church year. The four Sundays of Advent are a time to *prepare and wait in joyful hope.*

We prepare and wait to celebrate when Jesus, the Son of God, *came as a human being.*

We celebrate Jesus, the Son of God, *present in our midst* sharing his ministry with us.

We prepare, and wait in joyful hope for when Jesus, the Son of God, *returns in glory.* Are we ready to greet him?

Other Advent words are: *Be Alert, Be Ready, Be Awake!*

Advent is a time every year to ask questions.

In what condition is the stable of my heart? Do I say "no room here" or do I make room? Am I willing to say "Yes" to God, allowing Jesus to be born in my heart and willing to present him to the world? Am I ready to greet Jesus the King when he returns in glory?

Maranatha! Come, Lord Jesus!

CHRISTMAS

Advent ushers in the *Christmas Season* when we *celebrate God coming to his people as a baby, the word made flesh, Jesus.*

There are three parts to Christmas.

1. The Christmas experience, when God comes to us.
2. The Epiphany moment, when we recognize the truth of our Messiah and follow the light. We fall to our knees in adoration.
3. Baptism, which includes repentance, being renewed by the Spirit, and sent forth to live and proclaim the good news of Jesus.

The result of this threefold Christmas experience is conversion, a daily event of saying "yes" to our baptism. Conversion is an ongoing journey.

There are no studies for Christmas Day or Epiphany as it is a holiday time and people are gathering with family and friends. There is a study for Epiphany and the Baptism of our Lord. The Baptism of our Lord ends the Christmas season when we continue the routine of ordinary time.

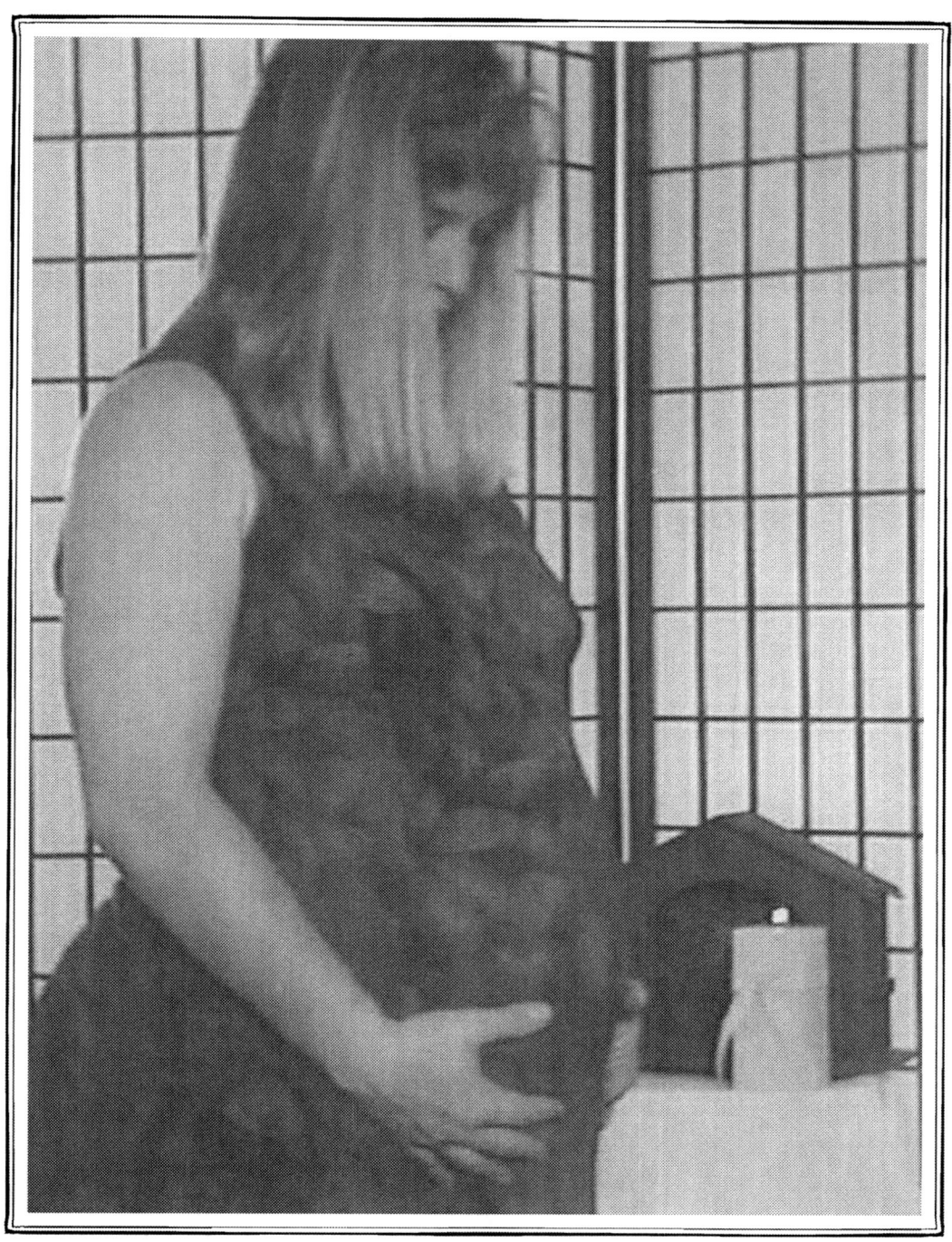

The angel said to her,
"The Holy Spirit will come upon you,
and the power of the Most High
will overshadow you;
therefore the Child to be born will be holy;
He will be called Son of God."

(Luke 1:35)

CHAPTER 16

FIRST SUNDAY OF ADVENT YEAR C

OPENING SONG
OPENING PRAYER

Open in prayer and invite everyone to add their own prayer. Close together: "Lead me in your truth and teach me, for you are the God of my salvation. Amen" (Psalm 25:5).

READ STUDY GUIDELINES

First Reading   Jeremiah 33:14-16

Setting the Stage

The first reading is from the book of the prophet Jeremiah. These words are spoken after the two tragic deportations of the Jews: the first is in 721 BC when the Assyrians captured the northern province of Israel, and the second is in the beginning of the sixth century BC when Babylonian armies conquered the southern province of Judah. God the Father, through these words, is encouraging his people by *renewing a promise he has made.* Note the expression "a righteous branch for David." This means "a good person belonging to the family tree of David." *Who is this good person to be?*

Read the first reading aloud. Reread this Scripture.
What word, phrase, or idea stands out for you?

COME TO ME

Exploring Further

1. In the days to come, what promise does God declare he will fulfill in Jeremiah 33:14-15?

2. What further insight is gained regarding this long-awaited promise?
   Isaiah 4: 2-3, 6
   Zechariah 6:12-13

3. What does Jesus say about how this promise will be fulfilled in Luke 21:25-28, Sunday's gospel?

4. What characterizes the rule of the "righteous Branch" according to the following?
   Jeremiah 33:15b
   Isaiah 11:1-5
   Psalm 72:1-5

5. What does God promise for Judah and Jerusalem in Jeremiah 33:16?

6. What shall this Branch be called according to the following?
   Jeremiah 33:16b
   Ezekiel 48:35b
   Matthew 1:21-23

Reflection

1. At a time when Jewish people were in captivity, God promises to bring justice and righteousness and safety. What promises of God give you hope for today?

2. This promise to the Jewish people was fulfilled in Jesus about six hundred years after it was made. How does God reassure you when his promises seem slow in coming?

3. What is one thing you have learned while waiting? Why is waiting valuable? What can be lost by not waiting?

Optional Exercise before the second reading. Have each person in the group briefly tell something of their past week or of an event anticipated in the coming week. This could be a time to share a triumph, a trial, or a need.

First Sunday of Advent Year C

Second Reading   1 Thessalonians 3:12- 4:2

Setting the Stage

This reading is from the first letter St. Paul wrote to the church in Thessalonika, Greece. Paul and his friends, Timothy and Silvanus, started the church there in AD 50. But there are people who do not like Paul and they run him out of town. Paul goes on to Athens, but is worried about his new converts in Thessalonika, so he sends Timothy back there to see how things are going. Timothy reports to Paul that the new Christians are persevering. St. Paul, inspired by the Holy Spirit, sends this letter—*it is the very first writing of the New Testament!* Note *the Advent theme: the coming of the Lord Jesus!*

Read the second reading aloud. Reread this Scripture.
What word, phrase, or idea stands out for you?

Exploring Further

1. What is Paul's prayer in 1 Thessalonians 3:12?

2. What practical ways can we grow in love and show love according to the following?
   Romans 12:17-21
   Galatians 6:10
   Titus 3:2

3. What is Paul's prayer and for what event in 1 Thessalonians 3:13?

4. What does Jesus say about being ready for his return in Luke 21:34-36, Sunday's gospel?

5. What further instructions on how to live are passed on in the following Scriptures?
   1 Thessalonians 4:1-3a
   Romans 12:1-2
   1 Corinthians 11:2

Reflection

These instructions are given to a people who are waiting in hope for the coming of the Lord. Do not repay evil, but respond with what is noble; as far as possible live peaceably with all; do not seek vengeance but leave vengeance to God; if your enemies are hungry feed them; if they are thirsty give them water; overcome evil with good; work for the good of all, especially the family of faith; speak evil of no one; avoid quarreling; be gentle and courteous; present your bodies as a living sacrifice, holy and blameless; be transformed by the renewing of your minds; maintain and remember the traditions of faith handed on to you; live as you know is right and avoid immorality; be on guard that you are not weighed down by food, drinking, and the worries of this life; be alert, pray for strength.

1. At Advent, we are reminded that we are a people waiting in hope for the coming of the Lord. Which of these ways to live and love do you need to implement at this time in your life?

2. What is one thing you can do (or continue to do) to grow in love and holiness this Advent?

3. How have you experienced support and hope through the prayers of others? Explain.

4. Paul prayed in 1 Thessalonians 3:12-13 that you may increase and abound in love for one another and may Jesus so strengthen your hearts in holiness that you will be blameless before God our Father at the coming of the Lord Jesus and all the saints. Who can you pray this prayer for today? Take a few minutes to pray this for those the group mentioned.

Closing Prayer

May the God of peace himself sanctify you entirely; and may our spirit, and soul, and body be kept sound and blameless at the coming of our Lord Jesus Christ. The one who has called you is faithful, and he will do this. Amen (1 Thessalonians 5:23-24).

CHAPTER 17

SECOND SUNDAY OF ADVENT
YEAR C

OPENING SONG
OPENING PRAYER

Open in prayer and invite everyone to add their own prayer. Close together: "Lord, remove the things that hinder us from receiving Christ with joy, so that we may share his wisdom and become one with him when he comes in glory. Amen."

REVIEW STUDY GUIDELINES

First Reading   **Baruch 5: 1-9 (See appendix one.)**

Setting the Stage

The first reading is from the book of the prophet Baruch. Baruch is the secretary of the famous prophet Jeremiah. However, the book of Baruch is written much later, about 250 BC. This is the time of bitter persecution against the Jewish people by Greek kings. This book is meant to be an encouragement to them. It does this by re-telling the story of the rescue of the Jewish people after their deportation and destruction of Jerusalem in 587 BC by an earlier enemy, the Babylonians. In this reading we hear about the restoration of Jerusalem after 500 BC. Note the phrase, "turn your eyes to the east." The east is a symbol of the dawn, a new and brighter day ahead! *In our moments of sorrow, to whom can we turn?*

Read the first reading aloud. Reread this Scripture.
What word, phrase, or idea stands out for you?

Come to Me

Exploring Further

1. What is Jerusalem asked to take off in Baruch 5:1a?

2. What does God want to replace this dress of sorrow with in Baruch 5:1b-2?

3. What does clothing symbolize in Isaiah 52:1 and Isaiah 61:10?

4. What messianic names are given to Jerusalem in Baruch 5:4?

5. What other messianic names are used in the following verses?
   Isaiah 1:26
   Isaiah 60:14
   Jeremiah 33:16

6. What hope and encouragement is given in Baruch 5:5-6?

7. How will God prepare the way for his people in Baruch 5:7?

8. How will God lead his people according to Isaiah 42:16?

9. How are God's people asked to prepare the way for the Lord and who is the messenger in Luke 3:2-6, Sunday's gospel?

10. How is John pre-announced?
    Isaiah 40:3-5
    Malachi 3:1
    Malachi 4:5-6 (or Malachi 3:23-24)
    Luke 1:5, 8-17

11. What does Jesus say about John the Baptist in Matthew 11:13-15?

12. What promise is given in Baruch 5:9?

Reflection

1. What robe of sorrow, misery, or pain are you wearing at this time in your life? How might you exchange this robe for God's cloak of justice, peace, strength, and joy?

2. God promises to gather back the children of Jerusalem and to smooth the way for their return. What hope does this give you for your loved ones who have strayed from faith?

Second Sunday of Advent Year C

3. What are some of the unexpected ways God has led you?

4. How can you prepare for the coming of the Lord at this time in your life?

Optional Exercise before the second reading. Have each person in the group briefly tell something of their past week or of an event anticipated in the coming week. This could be a time to share a triumph, a trial, or a need.

Second Reading — Philippians 1:4-6, 8-11

Setting the Stage

The second reading is from the letter of St. Paul to the church in Philippi, northern Greece. St. Paul establishes a church there in the year 50 AD and has many close friends. Six years later when they hear he is in a prison in southwestern Turkey, they send him help. Paul writes this letter to thank them. His prayer for them is also God our Father's wish for us. Note the Advent idea in the phrase, "the Day of Christ Jesus," which means "the coming of the Lord Jesus at the end of time."

Read the second reading aloud. Reread this Scripture.
What word, phrase, or idea stands out for you?

Exploring Further

1. What characterizes Paul's prayer in Philippians 1:4?

2. Why does he pray this way according to Philippians 1:5?

3. What is Paul confident of in Philippians 1:6?

4. What appears to be Paul's feeling toward these fellow Christians that he has worked with in spreading the gospel in Philippians 1:8?

5. What does Paul pray for the believers in Philippians 1:9?

6. How will this help them according to Philippians 1:10?

COME TO ME

7. What prayer or instruction is given the believer and for what purpose?

   Prayer or instruction **Purpose**

   Colossians 1:9-10
   Romans 12:2
   Ephesians 3:16-19
   Hebrews 5:7-7, 12-14
   Philemon 6

8. As we are filled with knowledge and insight, determining what is best, what does Jesus Christ produce in us according to Philippians 1:11?

9. From the following Scriptures, what results in spiritual growth and righteousness?
   John 15:7-8
   Hebrews 12:7, 10-11
   Ephesians 5:8-11

Reflection

1. Paul wrote with joy even though he was in prison. How do your circumstances affect your joy? Explain

2. Can you relate to joy in service? Explain. What bonds have you formed with people you have worked and prayed with while doing "kingdom work"? Explain.

3. Consider someone you think has a mature faith. What character qualities do you admire in this person? What in your life is helping you grow in spiritual maturity?

4. "The One who began a good work in you will go on completing it until the day of the Lord." What does this Scripture mean to you?

Closing Prayer

Come to us Lord. We rejoice in your presence and desire to serve you with all our hearts. Amen.

CHAPTER 18

THIRD SUNDAY OF ADVENT
YEAR C

OPENING SONG
OPENING PRAYER

Open in prayer and invite everyone to add their own prayer. Close together: "Rejoice in the Lord always; again I say, Rejoice. The Lord is near. Amen" (Philippians 4:4-5).

REVIEW STUDY GUIDELINES

First Reading   Zephaniah 3:14-18

Setting the Stage

The first reading is from the book of the prophet Zephaniah. Zephaniah lives about 650 years before Jesus, and works in the southern province of Judah. It is a difficult time because part of that province has been absorbed by the Assyrian Empire and there are a lot of religious disorders. Through these words, God our Father wants to encourage his people who, in this reading, are given four names: 1. Daughter of Zion, 2. Zion (Zion is the name of one of the hills on which Jerusalem is built.), 3. Daughter of Jerusalem, and 4. Israel. We can picture ourselves as having these names, and as we hear this message may it be a source of strength in our moments of sorrow.

Read the first reading aloud. Reread this Scripture.
What word, phrase, or idea stands out for you?

COME TO ME

Exploring Further

1. What are the people encouraged to do in Zephaniah 3:14?

2. What is the reason for rejoicing?
   Zephaniah 3:15
   Isaiah 40:2

3. What is pre-announced that will fulfill the above promise, in Zechariah 9:9?

4. What is said to Jerusalem in Zephaniah 3:16?

5. What does Jesus say in Matthew 14:27?

6. What image is used to represent God in Zephaniah 3:17a? What does this image imply or mean to you?

7. How will God display his love according to Zephaniah 17b-18?

8. Compare this image of God in question seven to the one used in Isaiah 62:5? What does this image say to you?

Reflection

1. This reading foretells of a time when the penalty and judgment for sin will be paid. We know this was fulfilled in the death and resurrection of Jesus. What does this mean to you? Does truth cause you to rejoice? Explain.

2. "Do not fear; do not let your hands grow weak." In what situation, now or in the past, have you experienced fear or discouragement? What difference does the promise that "God has removed your judgment" and that "the Lord your God is in your midst, a warrior who gives you victory," make in this situation?

3. Picture the Lord dancing with you; singing to you; gazing at you with eyes of love; whooping in delight over you. What is your reaction to the Lord loving and delighting in you in this way? Can you believe and receive this kind of love from the Lord? Explain.

Optional Exercise before the second reading. Have each person in the group briefly tell something of their past week or of an event anticipated in the coming week. This could be a time to share a triumph, a trial, or a need.

Third Sunday of Advent Year C

Second Reading   Philippians 4:4-7

Setting the Stage

The second reading is from the letter St. Paul writes to the Christians of Philippi, in northern Greece, about 25 years after the death and resurrection of Jesus. He is writing to thank them for their help and also to encourage them in their faith. (Paul is writing this letter from prison.) *As Christmas comes closer, these words of God our Father are very appropriate.*

Read the second reading aloud. Reread this Scripture.
What word, phrase, or idea stands out for you?

Exploring Further

1. What does Paul encourage believers to do in Philippians 4:4?

2. How are we to treat others and why, according to Philippians 4:5?

3. Because the "Lord is near," what else should we do according to 1 Peter 4:7-10?

4. "What must I do?" What practical advice does John give the people to prepare for the coming of Jesus in Luke 3:10-18, Sunday's gospel? How can this apply to us today?

5. What will repentance and a changed lifestyle prepare us to receive in Luke 3:16?

6. What are we told not to do in Philippians 4:6a?

7. Instead of worry, what should we do according to Philippians 4:6b?

8. What does Jesus say about worry in Matthew 6:25-34?

9. Philippians 4:6 says to make our request known *with thanksgiving*. What is said about giving thanks in Ephesians 5:20?

10. What is the result of turning to God with our needs according to Philippians 4:7?

11. What does Jesus promise when we turn to him in John 14:27?

Reflection

1. Since Paul was writing this from prison, it is obvious that rejoicing and trusting God for all we need rather than worrying is not dependent on our circumstances. Think of a circumstance in your life which is uncertain or rocky. How might you apply Paul's prescription of rejoice, don't worry, and ask with thanksgiving to your situation? Do you think joy is possible despite our circumstances? Why or why not?

2. Have you ever experienced "the peace of God that surpasses understanding"? Explain.

3. John encouraged the people to share and to be honest and just in their dealings with others. Paul says to rejoice, be gentle, pray, and ask with thanksgiving. How might you incorporate one or more of these actions to prepare your heart to receive the Lord?

4. The crowd, the tax collectors and the soldiers asked John, "What must I do?" Asking questions shows an awareness of need. Asking questions is the beginning of all learning. What heartfelt questions have you asked God or others on your spiritual journey that were a source of growth to you?

Advent Prayer Suggestion: In your prayer time from now until Christmas ask God, "At this point in my life what must I do?" Then listen for His response.

Closing Prayer

Lord, we rejoice in your goodness to us and we give you thanks in all things and for all things. Let your peace guard our hearts and minds. Amen.

CHAPTER 19

Fourth Sunday of Advent
Year C

Opening Song
Opening Prayer

Open in prayer and invite everyone to add their own prayer. Close together: "O Lord, our Shepherd, you bring down the powerful and raise up humble. We thank you for caring for us, your people. Amen."

Review Study Guidelines

First Reading   Micah 5:2-5 (or Micah 5:1-4a in some translations)

Setting the Stage

The first reading is from the book of the prophet Micah. Micah lives in the southern province of Judah about 700 years before Jesus. At this time there is a lot of social injustice: the wealthy are exploiting the poor and people are really not living their faith; they are just going through the motions. It is important to remember also that the Assyrian armies have reduced the Jewish kings to mere puppets, so the Jews are not free. God our Father, through Micah, condemns the misconduct of the people, but here speaks words of hope about the promised Messiah, and he gives the two names of the town that the Messiah would come from.

Read the first reading aloud. Reread this Scripture.
What word, phrase, or idea stands out for you?

Come to Me

Exploring Further

1. "Zedekiah is the last of the kings in David's line to sit on the throne in Jerusalem. Micah said that the next king in David's line would be the Messiah, who would establish a kingdom that would never end. Jerusalem's leaders were obsessed with wealth and position, but Micah prophesies that mighty Jerusalem, with all its wealth and power, would be besieged and destroyed.[28] In contrast to wealth and position, what is the promise to the tiny town of Bethlehem, in Micah 5:2?

2. How are these prophecies affirmed?
   Matthew 2:6
   John 7:42

3. When will this take place according to Micah 5:3? (or verse 2)

4. How is this sign they are waiting for clearly stated in Isaiah 7:14?

5. What is Elizabeth's response to this sign in Luke 1:41-45, Sunday's gospel?

6. How shall this ruler care for his people?
   Micah 5:4 (or verse 3)
   Isaiah 40:11

7. In the following Scriptures, what will be the result of this ruler coming?
   Micah 5:5a (or verse 4a)
   Jeremiah 33:15
   Ephesians 2:14

Reflection

1. Can you think of other examples in Scripture where the unexpected, outcast, weak, or little ones were used over the powerful, rich, educated, etc.? Can you think of examples when this was not the case? In history up until today who has God used in unexpected ways? What hope does this give you?

2. The coming of Jesus the Messiah was foretold. Elizabeth and John the Baptist recognized their fulfillment, yet most did not. When have you recognized God working in our midst? Was faith necessary to recognize this work? Explain.

3. When have you seen despair give birth to hope? What person made a difference in this process?

Optional Exercise before the second reading. Have each person in the group briefly tell something of their past week or of an event anticipated in the coming week. This could be a time to share a triumph, a trial, or a need.

Fourth Sunday of Advent Year C

Second Reading   Hebrews 10:5-10

Setting the Stage

The second reading is from the letter to the Hebrews, written about 40 years after the resurrection of Jesus. It is written by a Jew who has become a Christian and he is writing to other Jews who have become Christians but who are having a very difficult time. They are being persecuted and are tempted to go back to their old Jewish ways. The writer encourages them to persevere by showing how the Jewish Old Testament is a preparation for the coming of Jesus. In today's reading the writer portrays Jesus as actually quoting Psalm 40. This reading is like a short Bible study; he takes verses 6 to 8 of this psalm and explains them. The question being addressed is: *what, or rather* who *is the offering God our Father wants of us today?*

Read the second reading aloud. Reread this Scripture.
What word, phrase, or idea stands out for you?

Exploring Further

1. What does God desire?
   Hebrews 10:5-9a
   Psalm 40:6-8

2. What does God desire?
   1 Samuel 15:22
   Micah 6:6, 8

3. What do the following Scriptures say about the will and obedience of Jesus?
   Matthew 26:39, 42
   John 6:38
   John 10:17-18
   Do you think this is easy for Jesus to do? Why or why not?

4. What replaces the need of animal sacrifices and what is the result according to Hebrews 10:9b-10?

5. What effect should Jesus' sacrifice have on how we live?
   John 17:19
   Ephesians 5:1-2

Reflection

1. How do you understand the connection between growing in holiness and obedience?

2. Recall a recent incident when your will was different from someone you were working with or living with. Whose will prevailed and what was the result?

3. Can you recall a time when your will was different from God's will as revealed in Scripture and church teaching? Whose will prevails and what is the result?

4. Using concrete examples, discuss how we can offer our lives as a sacrifice to God. What result you have witnessed when people live in a sacrificial way? Who have you seen live a sacrificial life?

Closing Prayer

Lord, we are your servants. Let your will be done in our lives. Amen.

CHAPTER 20

BAPTISM OF OUR LORD YEAR C

OPENING SONG
OPENING PRAYER

Open in prayer and invite everyone to add their own prayer. Close together: "You are my beloved in whom I am well pleased. Amen."

REVIEW STUDY GUIDELINES

First Reading   Isaiah 40:1-5, 9-11

Setting the Stage

The first reading is from the book of the prophet Isaiah. These words are spoken about 540 years before Jesus when the Jewish people are being allowed to return to their homes 50 years after their deportation by Babylonian armies to what we know as Iraq. Note that the names "Jerusalem" and "Zion" were names given to all the Jewish people and that they have now become our names too. Through these words, God our Father is answering our question: *Who will help us in our rough moments to get our lives back together again?*

Read the first reading aloud. Reread this Scripture.
What word, phrase, or idea stands out for you?

Come to Me

Exploring Further

1. What is God's message to his people and why in Isaiah 40:1-2?

2. Why do the Israelites deserve enslavement and punishment—originally and then more recently—according to the following Scriptures?
   Genesis 2:15-17
   Genesis 3:6-7, 16-19, 23-24
   2 Kings 24:18-25:1, 4-7, 9-11

3. What promise is given to God's people?
   Isaiah 40:3-4
   Isaiah 49:13-17
   Malachi 3:23-24 (or Micah 4:5-6 in some translations)

4. How are these Scriptures fulfilled?
   Luke 1:13-17
   Luke 1:63-79
   Luke 3:15-16 (Sunday's gospel)

5. After the preparation, what will take place according to Isaiah 40:5?

6. How was God's glory revealed in the following Scriptures?
   Exodus 24:15-17
   John 1:14-15

7. What do the following Scriptures tell us about this "Word made flesh"?
   Psalm 119:89
   Matthew 24:35
   John 1:1
   1 Peter 1:23-25

8. What are the people instructed to do in Isaiah 40:9?

9. How will our God come according to Isaiah 40:10?

10. How does this power and authority come, as fulfillment to this prophesy, in Luke 3:21-22, Sunday's gospel?

11. What image of God is given in Isaiah 40:11?

Baptism of Our Lord Year C

12. What does the Lord say about the shepherds of Israel in Ezekiel 34:1-6?

13. What does God promise the people?
    Jeremiah 3:15
    Jeremiah 23:3-5

14. How is the promise of a Shepherd King fulfilled?
    Luke 15:4-7
    John 10:11-16

Reflection

1. Were you ever the cause of damage to another vehicle, ticketed for a traffic violation, in court for some crime, broke something belonging to someone else, the cause of a broken relationship? What were the consequences of your situation? Did anyone ever intervene and pay for you?

2. Do you see yourself as a "good" person who made a few mistakes or can you relate to Adam and Eve and the Israelites who deserved death and exile for their choices? Explain. Is receiving atonement for your guilt and an end to your exile from God through Jesus, head knowledge for you or is it an experiential truth? Explain.

3. In which way(s) do you relate to the Shepherd King—caring for you, seeking you out, rejoicing over you, laying down his life for you, protecting you, hearing his voice, other? Explain.

4. God the Father made the same proclamation at your baptism as he did at Jesus' baptism. Have each person read aloud the following sentence. "You are my child (insert your name) the beloved; with you I am well pleased."

Optional Exercise before the second reading. Have each person in the group briefly tell something of their past week or of an event anticipated in the coming week. This could be a time to share a triumph, trial, or a need.

Come to Me

Second Reading   Titus 2:11-14; 3:4-7

Setting the Stage

The second reading is from the letter of St. Paul to Titus. Titus is a close friend and co-worker of Paul whom Paul has put in charge of the Christians on the island of Crete. These words are meant to help leaders of churches. Through these words God our Father speaks to us about the past appearances and the future appearances of his Son in our world. *What difference do they make for us? How do they impact on us?*

Read the second reading aloud. Reread this Scripture.
What word, phrase, or idea stands out for you?

Exploring Further

1. What does God offer and desire for all people?
   Titus 2:11
   1 Timothy 2:3-4

2. What does God's grace do for us and what are we waiting for according to Titus 2:12-13?

3. What does God do for us in 2 Corinthians 1:21-22?

4. What is the state of the human race without God?
   Titus 3:3
   Romans 3:23

5. What is God's plan from the beginning of time?
   Exodus 19:5
   Deuteronomy 7:6
   Psalm 130:8

6. What does Jesus do for us?
   Titus 2:14; 3:4-5a
   Romans 3:24
   1 Timothy 1:12-16

Baptism of Our Lord Year C

7. How does Jesus save us and what is the sign given in these Scriptures?
   Titus 3:5b-6
   John 3:3, 5, 8
   Acts 2:38-39
   Romans 6:4
   Ephesians 5:25-26

8. What does Jesus receive at baptism and what does he do after his baptism according to Luke 3:22-23a?

9. Through baptism, what does God call us to?
   Titus 3:7
   2 Timothy 1:9

Reflection

1. From the above Scriptures God's plan is that all people come to salvation; that we be a holy people, his chosen, treasured possession; that we receive our inheritance and eternal life. We learn from the above Scriptures that baptism plays a central part in this plan. How would you describe the role of baptism, God's part and our part in God's plan?

2. From the above Scriptures we discover that through faith and baptism we are: redeemed, purified, saved and justified; we are given a new birth, life, a living hope, and made heirs and children of God; we are made holy, strengthened, called for service, and empowered. When all this has been done for us, why do you think so many baptized do not practice their faith and so often live our faith poorly?

3. There are three great feasts in the Christmas season. First we celebrate Christmas—God coming to us. Second is Epiphany; we seek truth, recognize truth, and worship. Third is the baptism of our Lord; we repent, believe, and are sent forth to proclaim and live out the good news. This is also a summary of conversion. Conversion is not a one time event but a lifelong ongoing process. Can you think of examples of this process in your life? Explain. What are practical things we can do to ensure we are part of this conversion process? What things might short-circuit this process?

4. At his baptism Jesus was empowered to begin his ministry and fulfill his mission. At your baptism you were empowered for ministry and to fulfill God's mission for you. "Having become a member of the church, the person baptized belongs no longer to himself, but to him who died and rose for us. From now on, he is called to be subject to others and to serve them in the communion of the church. Baptism is a source of responsibilities and duties as well as rights within the church. Reborn as sons of God, [the baptized] must profess before men the faith they have received from

God through the church and participate in the apostolic and missionary activity of the People of God."[29] What is your response to the idea that God has a mission and ministry for you to fulfill? In your life now, how are you professing your faith before others and participating in the apostolic and missionary activity of the People of God?

Closing Prayer

Lord, in your mercy you have delivered us, cleansed us, and empowered us. May we receive your gift of life with faith and become your children in name and in fact. Amen.

CHAPTER 21

Epiphany of the Lord
Year C

Opening Song
Opening Prayer

Open in prayer and invite everyone to add their own prayer. Close together: "King and savior, you are the light and truth made manifest to all nations. Lord, please grant us an encounter of this revelation in our lives today. Amen."

Review Study Guidelines

First Reading Isaiah 60:1-6

Setting the Stage

The first reading is from the book of the prophet Isaiah. These words are spoken about 540 years before Jesus. The Jewish people have been conquered 50 years earlier by the Babylonians; Jerusalem has been destroyed and many are deported to Babylon, which is Iraq today. However, the Babylonians are conquered by the Persian Empire whose foreign policy is very different; they allow conquered peoples to have their own customs, religion, and to live in their own country. So the deported Jews are going home at last. This reading is a poem addressed to the people of Jerusalem who have been left there when the deportations took place. We shall be hearing in this reading the ancient names for Arabia, Ethiopia, and Spain. Listen for a hint of the Story of the Three Wise Men. Through these words God our Father tells us *who are called to be his people; would it be only certain ones, or....*

Come to Me

Read the first reading aloud. Reread this Scripture.
What word, phrase, or idea stands out for you?

Exploring Further

1. What is promised to the Israelites?
   Isaiah 60:1-2
   Numbers 24:17

2. How will other nations be affected by this promise?
   Isaiah 60:3
   Isaiah 42:1, 4, 6
   Micah 4:1-3

3. How is the rising of a star that leads other nations fulfilled in Matthew 2:1-9, Sunday's gospel?

4. What is promised to Israel from the following Scriptures?
   Isaiah 60:4
   Baruch 5:5-6 (See appendix one.)

5. How will Israel be honored by other nations?
   Isaiah 60:5-6
   Psalm 72:10-11

6. How is the promise of nations bringing wealth and paying homage fulfilled in Matthew 2:10-11?

7. The gift of gold represents royalty; frankincense represents divinity, and myrrh indicates passion or suffering. In presenting gold, frankincense, and myrrh to Jesus, what are the wise men indicating about this baby in the stable?

8. After the star leads the wise men to Jesus and they pay homage and present gifts, what follows in the narrative in Matthew 2:12?

Reflection

1. Jesus is the light promised to all nations. Epiphany is the manifestation of God to all peoples. What is the truth Jesus brings that transcends all time, all nations, and all cultures to meet the need of every human heart? How is the gospel message misrepresented when people's dignity and culture are not respected? How can this poor representation of the gospel message be avoided?

Epiphany of the Lord Year C

2. Isaiah speaks of the overflowing joy in Israel in seeing their sons and daughters return from captivity. What things today place people in captivity? Can you relate to the joy of being freed from captivity in your life or in seeing someone else's life healed and transformed? Explain.

3. The wise men presented Jesus with gifts or treasure. What gifts or treasure do you have to present Jesus directly or to present to Jesus by giving them to others?

4. After the wise men's encounter with the living God, they returned home by a different route. After searching and encountering Jesus, we are never the same. How has your life taken a different route since an encounter with the living God?

Optional Exercise before the second reading. Have each person in the group briefly tell something of their past week or of an event anticipated in the coming week. This could be a time to share a triumph, a trial, or a need.

Second Reading   Ephesians 3:2a, 5-6

Setting the Stage

The second reading is from the letter of Paul to the Ephesians. This is a circular letter to the Christians living around Ephesus, a city in what is now southwestern Turkey. Scholars are uncertain about the actual author; it is either Paul or one of his followers who, under the inspiration of the Holy Spirit, takes Paul's thoughts and life experiences and records them under Paul's name toward the end of the first century AD. In any case, these are God our Father's words and He tells us about St. Paul who is a very fervent Jew and who is touched by Jesus about six years after His resurrection. We hear *why this happens*.

Read this reading aloud. Reread this Scripture.
What word, phrase, or idea stands out for you?

Exploring Further

1. What is Paul reminding his listeners of in Ephesians 3:2?

2. What is Paul's commission in Ephesians 3:7-8?

3. How does Paul receive revelation of this mystery in Acts 26:12-18?

4. How is this mystery revealed according to Ephesians 3:5? (or verses 4-5)

5. What does the mystery of the gospel being revealed mean to the Gentiles?
   Ephesians 3:6
   Ephesians 3:12-13, 19

6. Who does God share the mystery of Jesus' birth with?
   Matthew 2:1-2, 9-11, Sunday's gospel
   Luke 2:8-16
   Luke 2:25-32

7. What should be a guiding star for us according to 2 Peter 1:16-19?

Reflection

1. Paul is commissioned to bring the mystery of the gospel to the Gentiles so that all people can share in the promises of Jesus Christ. In your life, what have you been commissioned to do or given the privilege of doing for the sake of the gospel?

2. The prophets and apostles are given revelation of the mystery of the gospel by the Holy Spirit. God first reveals the birth of Jesus to the shepherds, the wise men who are strangers and foreigners, and to Simeon. What characteristics do these people have that make them open to God's revelation? What attitudes should we develop to be fertile soil to receive from God?

3. The wise men followed the star that led them to Jesus. What is your star that led you, or is leading you, to Jesus?

Closing Prayer

Lord, thank you for making it possible for us to share in all the promises of Jesus Christ. Give us the grace to seek and follow the stars you lead us by. Amen.

SECTION THREE

ORDINARY TIME AFTER CHRISTMAS

The baptism of Jesus ends the Christmas season and we are back into the routine of ordinary time.

Remember that ordinary time is an ideal time to develop a solid foundation and a relationship with the Father, Son, and Holy Spirit that will prepare us for the times of celebration as well as the times of sorrow.

Easter is a moveable feast day which means the number of Sundays of Ordinary Time between now and Lent varies from five to nine. At the Council of Nicaea in 325 AD, all churches agreed that Easter should be celebrated on the first Sunday after the first full moon after the spring equinox.[30] Watch for the first Sunday of Lent.

*And these are the ones sown on the good soil:
they hear the word and accept it
and bear fruit, thirty and sixty
and a hundred-fold.*

(Mark 4:20)

CHAPTER 22

Second Sunday of Ordinary Time Year C

Opening Song
Opening Prayer

Open in prayer and invite everyone to add their own prayer. Close together: "At the beginning of this week of Christian unity, Lord, we pray that, just as you transformed water into wine, transform us into one, holy people. Amen."

Review Study Guidelines

## First Reading	Isaiah 62: 1-5

Setting the Stage

The first reading is from the book of the prophet Isaiah written around 540 years before Jesus. The Jewish people are being allowed to return home again after being deported to Babylon (now known as Iraq) about 50 years earlier. The Babylonians have completely destroyed Jerusalem which is also known as Zion. The work of rebuilding will be long and frustrating. But while others are becoming miserable and small-minded, this writer breaks into song over the city that will become alive again. The names Jerusalem and Zion have become our names, and so these words of God our Father are meant for us in our moments of pain and discouragement.

Read the first reading aloud. Reread this Scripture.

COME TO ME

What word, phrase, or idea stands out for you?

Exploring Further

1. In Isaiah's zeal for his people he says he will not be silent or rest until when, according to Isaiah 62:1?

2. What is prophesied to happen in Isaiah 62:2?

3. "A proper name defines the nature of the being that bears it, and fixes its destiny. A change of name signifies a change of vocation. cf. Abraham. Gn. 17:5; Israel Gn 32:29; etc. The Jerusalem of the future was to receive other prophetic names."[31] By what names is Jerusalem known at this time in Isaiah 62:4a?

4. What names will Jerusalem be known by in the future?
   Isaiah 62:4b, 12
   Isaiah 60:14
   Isaiah 1:26
   Ezekiel 48:35

5. What is God's promise to his people in Isaiah 62:5?

6. How is the transformation of Jerusalem from desolate and forsaken to married and delighted in, symbolized in John 2:1-2, 6-12, Sunday's gospel, and where does this event take place?

7. Besides the literal meaning of Mary's words, how might they sum up the spiritual state of God's people and what might wine symbolize in John 2:3?

8. What is Mary's instruction that is applicable to all who would enter into transformation in John 2:5?

Reflection

1. What is the meaning of your name? Do you know why your parents choose your name(s)? How did you choose names for your children? Have you ever had a name change? Explain.

2. What significance is there in a woman taking her husband's name at marriage? Do you think this reflects a change in vocation? Why or why not?

3. The image of marriage is often used to express God's relationship to his people. How do you picture your marriage relationship to God? In your prayer life, do you pray to the Father, Son, Holy Spirit, or all three? Has this changed over the years? Explain.

Second Sunday of Ordinary Time Year C

4. Is there any issue you continuously and unrelentingly bring before God and will not rest until it is accomplished? How does this affect your prayer life?

Optional Exercise before the second reading. Have each person in the group briefly tell something of their past week or of an event anticipated in the coming week. This could be a time to share a triumph, trial, or a need.

Second Reading   1 Corinthians 12:4-11

Setting the Stage

The next reading is from the first letter St. Paul writes to the church in Corinth, Greece, about 25 years after the resurrection of Jesus. One of the problems in the Corinthian church is disorderly conduct during Mass. Through these words God our Father speaks to us about the *many gifts he has given and what they are meant to do.*

Note the "gift of tongues." This is the most mysterious of the gifts. It is an ability to pray and praise God our Father by making sounds that are continuous and in syllables, but not intelligible. In this reading the name "God" refers to God the Father and the name "Lord" refers to Jesus; notice, then, the mention of the Blessed Trinity.

Read the second reading aloud. Reread this Scripture.
What word, phrase, or idea stands out for you?

Exploring Further

1. How is the Trinity referred to in 1 Corinthians 12:4-6?

2. What three areas are mentioned as having variety or differences and what is the same in each area according to 1 Corinthians 12:4-6?

3. Why are the manifestations of the Spirit given according to 1 Corinthians 12:7?

4. What are the manifestations of the Spirit listed in 1 Corinthians 12:8-10?

5. What gifts of the Spirit are listed in Romans 12:6-8?

6. Which manifestation of the spiritual gifts is mentioned in the following Scriptures?
   John 2:7-9a
   Acts 2:4
   Acts 6:9-10
   Acts 3:6-8
   Acts 11:27-28
   1 John 4:1-3

7. Who chooses who will manifest these gifts according to 1 Corinthians 12:11?

Reflection

1. The Corinthian church is split because of spiritual gifts. Why do you think this might have happened? How might division and rivalry over spiritual gifts be avoided?

2. God gives spiritual gifts for the building up of the body. Do you think we must be open and available vessels in order to be used by God? Why or why not?

3. Would you describe yourself as available, avoiding being used, unaware you could even be used by God, other? Explain.

Closing Prayer

Lord, fill us with your Spirit and make us one in peace and love. Amen.

CHAPTER 23

Third Sunday of Ordinary Time Year C

Opening Song
Opening Prayer

Open in prayer and invite everyone to add their own prayer. Close together: "Lord, your law is perfect, reviving the soul; the precepts of the Lord are right, rejoicing the heart. Amen" (Psalm 19:7a, 8a).

Review Study Guidelines

First Reading   Nehemiah 8:1-4a, 5-6, 8-10

Setting the Stage

The first reading is from the book of Nehemiah. Nehemiah, who lives about 450 years before Jesus, is a Jew who has, under the conquering Persian king, become the governor of Judah. The capital, Jerusalem, has been destroyed by the Babylonian army 100 years earlier and the work of reconstruction of the city and the culture is slow. Nehemiah is very anxious to see the people return to the full practice of their faith and is aided in his efforts by a priest named Ezra. We hear now what happens to the people when God our Father's word is spoken to them. Note the expression "the book of the law." This refers to the first five books of the Bible. Note also that these books are written in Hebrew, but the Jewish people at this time speak only Aramaic. They are seen weeping. This is an expression of their sorrow for their failure to follow the word of the Lord. We can ask ourselves: *Can God's Word have a place in my life, in my daily struggles?* The people were gathering to celebrate.

Come to Me

Read the first reading aloud. Then reread asking, "What am I hearing in this reading?"
Write a word, a phrase, or an idea that stands out for you.

Exploring Further

1. Who is the scribe mentioned in Nehemiah 8:1?

2. What else do we learn about Ezra in Ezra 7:6?
   Note: the scribe is the man who reads, translates, and expounds the Law to God's people. Ezra is the father of these scribes who did much good work in the post-exilic period, which was continued by the scribes of the time of Christ.[32]

3. Who is gathered to listen to the book of the law, how do they listen, and for how long, according to Nehemiah 8:3?

4. What do you think the attitude and frame of mind of the people is in Nehemiah 8:5-6?

5. What is significant in Nehemiah 8:8 and why?

6. What is the response of the people and why do you think this is so in Nehemiah 8:9?

7. What is the response of the people to Jesus reading in the temple in Luke 4:15-21, 29, Sunday's gospel?
   Note: At the synagogue, the leader could invite a visiting rabbi to read from the Scriptures and to teach.[33]

8. What does Ezra tell the people to do in Nehemiah 8:10-12 and why?

9. How are those who have nothing able to join the celebration?

Reflection

1. Have you ever heard or read God's Word and it spoke right to your heart? Did this: cause you to repent, have hope, experience joy, move you to action, bring healing, or other? Have you ever had someone teach on a Scripture, opening it up for you and giving you new insights and understanding? Explain. What effect did this have on you?

2. The people in today's reading listen attentively, with reverence and worship. Today, what is the attitude in the community when the Word is read? How well do you listen? What cultural factors might affect our listening abilities?

Third Sunday of Ordinary Time Year C

3. Do you think sharing with others enhances celebration? Why or why not?

Optional Exercise before the second reading. Have each person in the group briefly tell something of their past week or of an event anticipated in the coming week. This could be a time to share a triumph, trial, or a need.

Second Reading — 1 Corinthians 12:12-30

Setting the Stage

The next reading is from the first letter that St. Paul wrote to the church in Corinth, Greece, about 25 years or so after the resurrection of Jesus. Reports have come to Paul that there is disorderly conduct when the Corinthian Christians meet for Eucharist. In response Paul draws a beautiful comparison between church and the human body. Through these words of Paul, God our Father tells us here *what a church is meant to look like.*

Read the second reading aloud. Reread this Scripture.
What word, phrase, or idea stands out for you?

Exploring Further

1. What makes us one body according to 1 Corinthians 12:12-13?

2. Who makes up the body of Christ according to 1 Corinthians 12:12-13?

3. In this analogy, what represents members' thinking they have nothing to give to the body in 1 Corinthians 12:14-16? How does this happen in the church body today?

4. What represents pride and thinking they are all that is needed in 1 Corinthians 12:21?

5. How does this happen in the church body today?

6. Who assigns each person their role in the body according to 1 Corinthians 12:18?

7. How are the weaker and less respected members treated in 1 Corinthians 12:22-24?

8. How might this apply to the body of Christ and how are these members indispensable?

9. What should the relationships within the body be according to 1 Corinthians 12:25-26?

10. What are some functions of the body as listed in 1 Corinthians 12:27-30?

11. What functions of the body are listed in Ephesians 4:11?

12. What is the purpose for these functions according to Ephesians 4:12-13?

13. What does Paul encourage in 1 Corinthians 12:31?

14. What is the better way according to 1 Corinthians 13:1-3?

Reflection

1. How does having the person on your right regularly attending this study make the whole group more effective?

2. How does having members of the body not coming together with the larger church affect the body?

3. "If one member suffers, all suffer." Who do you know that is suffering? How can you respond? How have people supported you in times of suffering?

4. What are some reactions you have had when someone in your church community has been honored? How have others rejoiced with you?

Closing Prayer

Father, may the life you give us increase our love for one another and bring us into unity and joy of your kingdom. Amen.

CHAPTER 24

Fourth Sunday of Ordinary Time Year C

Opening Song
Opening Prayer

Open in prayer and invite everyone to add their own prayer. Close together: "Lord, you are my hope and my trust. I have learned from birth. You are my rock and refuge. Amen."

Review Study Guidelines

First Reading   Jeremiah 1:4-5, 17-19

Setting the Stage

The first reading gives us the opening words of the book of the prophet Jeremiah. When God our Father calls him to be a prophet in the year 626 BC,[34] Jeremiah is only a very young man, perhaps 19 or 20 years of age. He describes his call here. *God our Father tells us what he promised Jeremiah and what he promises to all those who speak in his name.*

Read the first reading aloud. Reread this Scripture.
What word, phrase, or idea stands out for you?

Exploring Further

Note: To 'know', when said of God, means to choose and predestine. To 'consecrate' means not so much inward sanctification as a setting apart for prophetic ministry.[35]

Come to Me

1. When is Jeremiah called by God and what is he consecrated for, according to Jeremiah 1:4-5?

2. When is Isaiah called by God and what is he consecrated for, according to Isaiah 49:1?

3. When is John called and what is he consecrated for, according to Luke 1:14-17?

4. When is Paul called and what is he consecrated for, according to Galatians 1:15?

5. What truth for all people is stated in Psalm 139:14-16?

6. What are we each called for, according to Ephesians 2:10?

7. What objection does Jeremiah make and what is God's response in Jeremiah 1:6-7?

8. What does God tell Jeremiah to do in Jeremiah 1:17?

9. What do we learn about the importance of speaking what God shows us, in Ezekiel 3:16-19?

10. What does God say will be the likely response when Jeremiah speaks God's word in Jeremiah 1:19a?

11. What does Jesus say to the people of his home town and how do they respond in Luke 4:22-30, Sunday's gospel?

12. What is God's promise in Jeremiah 1:18-19?

Reflection

1. Do you believe you were called by God before you were born? Why or why not? Do you believe God has chosen you for a special work? Explain.

2. What objections have you used to try and get out of doing what it appears God is setting before you to do?

3. How have you experienced God being with you as you attempted to be obedient to what God has set before you to do?

4. At times God's Word is comforting and at times it convicts us, calling us to humbly submit to God's Word and way. What word of God is convicting to our society and culture today? What is the response?

Fourth Sunday of Ordinary Time Year C

Optional Exercise before the second reading. Have each person in the group briefly tell something of their past week or of an event anticipated in the coming week. This could be a time to share a triumph, trial, or a need.

Second Reading   1 Corinthians 12:31–13:13

Setting the Stage

The next reading is from the first letter that St. Paul writes to the church in Corinth, Greece, about 25 years after the resurrection of Jesus. One of the problems in the Corinthian church is that they are using some of their spiritual gifts in disorderly ways at their services. In response, Paul is inspired by the Holy Spirit to write one of the most sublime passages of the entire Bible.

1. To "speak in tongues" is an ability to pray and praise God our Father by making sounds that are continuous and in syllables, but not intelligible.[36]
2. "Prophecy" is the word of the Lord…the living word of a living God, not archival record. Prophecy is new insights into the mystery of salvation.[37]
3. The expression to "hand over my body" means voluntary self-immolation, that is, a giving over of one's very life.[38]

Through these words God our Father tells us *what the most important gift is that the Holy Spirit brings to humans.*

Read this reading aloud. Reread this Scripture.
What word, phrase, or idea stands out for you?

Exploring Further

1. What do the spiritual gifts amount to if not used in love? List the spiritual gifts mentioned in 1 Corinthians 13:1-3.

2. How does Jesus express a similar sentiment in Matthew 7:21-23?

3. How does Paul present this truth in James 2:14-17?

4. List the virtues of love in 1 Corinthians 13:4-7 and how each quality of love is directed toward others.

5. Could someone grow in love without living and working with other people? Why or why not?

6. What practical advice about love is given in the following Scriptures?
   Romans 12:9-13
   Romans 13:9
   1 Thessalonians 5:14-15
   Proverbs 10:12

7. What do we learn about love in 1 Corinthians 13:8a?

8. How will these gifts change and why, according to 1 Corinthians 13:8b-11?

9. What do we learn from 1 Corinthians 13:12?

10. How is this image further expanded in 1 John 3:2?

11. What are the three virtues mentioned in 1 Corinthians 13:13? Why do you think love is the greatest?

Reflection

1. Have each person read 1 Corinthians 13:4-7 putting their own names in place of love. When reading these verses where do you feel the most growth is needed for you?

2. Since love is the most important thing for eternity, how can we grow in love?

3. In *The Gift of Peace,* by Joseph Cardinal Bernadin, Cardinal Bernadin tells of spending hours leafing through his mother's photo album of Italy as she would tell him stories of the people and places in each picture. When he made his first trip to Tonadico he was surprised he knew the mountains, the land, the houses and the people. Because of the photos he knew this place and felt at home. Cardinal Bernadin expressed his belief that crossing from this life into eternal life will be a similar experience.

If you were to die today, how familiar do you think heaven would seem to you: A. like the home you are waiting for? B. slightly familiar? C. like a place someone once described to you? D. a foreign country? E. other? Explain. What is one thing you can start to do or continue doing so that heaven will be familiar territory when you arrive?

Closing Prayer

Lord, fill our hearts with your love that it may overflow to others. Amen.

CHAPTER 25

PRESENTATION OF THE LORD
ONLY WHEN SUNDAY FALLS ON FEBRUARY 2ND

OPENING SONG
OPENING PRAYER

Open in prayer and invite everyone to add their own prayer. Close together: "Lord, create in me a clean heart, O God, and put a new and right spirit within me. The sacrifice acceptable to God is a broken contrite spirit; a broken and contrite heart, O God, you will not despise. Amen." (Psalm 51:10, 17).

REVIEW STUDY GUIDELINES

First Reading   Malachi 3:1-4

Setting the Stage

The first reading is from the book of the prophet Malachi. Malachi is not a name; it is the Hebrew word for "My messenger," and we know only a little of the messenger who wrote this part of the Bible. He lives about 500 years before Jesus, and he loves his Jewish faith so much that he is not afraid to criticize the "descendents of Levi" who are the Jewish priests and temple assistants and who are insincere in their work in the temple. These words are appropriately chosen for this feast of the Presentation of the Lord; we hear *what a difference Christ will make in the temple.*

Read the first reading aloud. Reread this Scripture.
What word, phrase, or idea stands out for you?

Come to Me

Exploring Further

1. Who is God sending and for what purpose according to Malachi 3:1a?

2. Who is this messenger according to Malachi 3:23? (Malachi 4:5 in some translations.)

3. What does Jesus say about this messenger?
    Matthew 11:10-15
    Matthew 17:11-13

4. What is foretold about John the Baptist in Luke 1:11-13, 17?

5. After the way is prepared, who will enter the temple, and how, according to Malachi 3:1?

6. How does the Lord enter the temple according to Luke 2:22-24?

7. How is the coming of Jesus to the temple announced in Luke 2:25-38, Sunday's gospel?

8. What image of the Lord's coming is given in Malachi 3:2-3?

9. What do we learn of this purifying process from the following Scriptures?
    Ezekiel 22:18-22
    Daniel 12:10
    Matthew 3:10-12
    Luke 2:33-35

10. What are some things we need to be purified from in Malachi 3:5?

11. What will follow this purification according to Malachi 3:3b-4?

12. What type of sacrifice does God desire according to Psalm 51:17?

13. What sacrifice do we share in for the forgiveness of our sins in Hebrews 10:8-10?

Reflection

1. Who has been a "messenger" in your life preparing the way for experiencing God in a deeper way or who has been an instrument to show you your need to repent?

2. God wants to refine and purify our hearts. In what ways might this process be accomplished?

Presentation of the Lord (Only When Sunday Falls on February 2nd)

3. When the King of Glory enters the temple as a baby only Anna and Simeon recognize him. How can we be alert to the presence of Jesus? What may cause us to not recognize his presence?

4. Simeon declared he could die in peace now that he had seen the Lord. What would produce fulfillment and peace for you in old age?

Optional Exercise before the second reading. Have each person in the group briefly tell something of their past week or of an event anticipated in the coming week. This could be a time to share a triumph, a trial, or a need.

Second Reading   Hebrews 2:10-11, 13b-18

Setting the Stage

The next reading is from the letter to the Hebrews written by a Jewish Christian to other Jewish Christians about 40 years after the resurrection of Jesus. He often quotes from the Old Testament (and here we have a text from the prophet Isaiah). This is to show that everything in the Jewish faith points to Jesus and to be a Christian, then, is to be a descendant of Abraham. Through this reading, God our Father tells us *why Jesus became a human being and the price he paid in doing that.*

Read the second reading aloud. Reread this Scripture.
What word, phrase, or idea stands out for you?

Exploring Further

1. Why does Jesus become human (flesh and blood) according to Hebrews 2:14-15?

2. What power does Satan have according to the following Scriptures?
   Hebrews 2:14
   2 Corinthians 4:4
   1 John 5:18-19

3. What does Jesus do to Satan's power and dominion according to the following?
   Colossians 1:13-14
   2 Timothy 1:10

Come to Me

4. Who does Jesus come to free according to Hebrews 2:16?

5. What promise does this fulfill in Isaiah 41:8-10?

6. Why did Jesus become like us?
   Hebrews 2:17
   Hebrews 4:15
   1 John 2:2

7. How is Jesus tested and why, according to Hebrews 2:18?

8. How is Jesus tempted to seek nourishment apart from God and how does he respond in Matthew 4:1-4?

9. How is Jesus tempted to self-indulgence and what is his response in Matthew 4:5-6?

10. How is Jesus tempted to serve the powers of this world and what is his response in Matthew 4:8-10?

11. Why would God test according to the following?
    Exodus 16:4
    Deuteronomy 8:16
    2 Chronicles 32:31
    Jeremiah 11:20

12. How is temptation usually initiated according to the following?
    1 Thessalonians 3:5
    1 Timothy 6:9
    James 1:13-14
    Revelation 2:10

13. What is helpful to remember in times of suffering and testing?
    1 Corinthians 10:13
    1 Peter 1:6-7

Reflection

1. What does it mean to you that the power of death is destroyed?

2. How has someone's experience of suffering been an example or an encouragement to you or given you hope in your time of suffering?

Presentation of the Lord (Only When Sunday Falls on February 2nd)

3. What are common ways we are: Tempted to seek nourishment apart from God? Tempted to self-indulgence? Tempted to follow false gods who serve the powers of this world?

4. What have you learned through suffering? How has suffering strengthened you or changed you?

Closing Prayer

Lord, we are grateful that you have shared in all our sufferings and will help us when we are tested. Give us wisdom and grace to support others in their time of suffering. Help us always to turn to you and trust your promise that you will not give us more than we can bear. Amen.

CHAPTER 26
Fifth Sunday of Ordinary Time Year C

Opening Song
Opening Prayer

Open in prayer and invite everyone to add their own prayer. Close together: "Lord, we pray you will touch our hearts and lips with your divine presence. Amen."

Review Study Guidelines

First Reading   Isaiah 6:1-2a, 3-8

Setting the Stage

The first reading is from the book of the prophet Isaiah and tells us how God our Father calls him to be a prophet. In fact, he gives the date of his call using these words, "the year that King Uzziah [the king of Judah] died," which was 740 BC. Note these words:
1. Lord of hosts means Lord of power and might.
2. Seraph is the Hebrew word for angel.

Note also that in the Bible smoke is a sign of God our Father's presence and we see *how he responds to Isaiah's sense of unworthiness.*

Read the first reading aloud. Reread this Scripture.
What word, phrase, or idea stands out for you?

Come to Me

Exploring Further

1. Describe what Isaiah saw in Isaiah 6:1-3.
   A note of interest: Each [Seraph] has six wings. Reverence for the divine majesty causes them to veil their faces with two wings; modesty, to veil their extremities in similar fashion; alacrity in God's service, to extend two wings in preparation for flight.[39]

2. What happens in Isaiah 6:4?

3. What does smoke or clouds symbolize as seen in the following Scriptures?
   Exodus 19:16
   Exodus 40:34-35
   Revelation 15:8

4. What is Isaiah's response to this scene in Isaiah 6:5?

5. What might the reason for Isaiah's exclamation of woe be, considering Exodus 33:19?

6. What is the result of Isaiah's confession in Isaiah 6:6-7?
   Note of interest: Isaiah is thus symbolically purified to be worthy of his vocation as God's prophet. In the Roman liturgy, the celebrant at Mass makes reference to this incident just before he reads the gospel.[40]

7. After Isaiah's "God experience," what is his call or mission and how does Isaiah respond in Isaiah 6:8-9a?

8. What similarities to Isaiah's experience are in the following Scriptures?
   Jeremiah 1:4-10
   Daniel 10:16-19
   Luke 5:1-11 (Sunday's gospel)

Reflection

1. Consider Isaiah's vision. The Lord on a throne, high and lofty, angels all about singing so as the shake the temple; smoke filling the room... What might your response be to this experience? What does it say to you about the Lord and about heaven?

2. How have you experienced God touching you? Can you relate to Isaiah or Simon's experience of seeing their own sinfulness and then receiving God's forgiveness and mercy? Explain.

3. Can you relate to being asked to do something that you did not feel capable of and God giving you the grace to do it? Explain.

Fifth Sunday of Ordinary Time Year C

Optional Exercise before the second reading. Have each person in the group briefly tell something of their past week or of an event anticipated in the coming week. This could be a time to share a triumph, trial, or a need.

Second Reading 1 Corinthians 15:1-11

Setting the Stage

The next reading is from the first letter that St. Paul writes to the church in Corinth, Greece, about 25 years after the resurrection of Jesus. A big problem for the Corinthian Christians comes from Greek philosophy: the human body does not have any value after death—only the soul matters. Thus the resurrection of Jesus is put in question. In response, Paul speaks about his own conversion experience and mentions a man called "Cephas;" this is Aramaic for St. Peter. Through these words, God our Father tells us the *good news of his risen Son's presence among us.*

Read this reading aloud. Reread this Scripture.
What word, phrase, or idea stands out for you?

Exploring Further

1. What three distinct steps to passing on the good news are mentioned in 1 Corinthians 15:1?

2. What must we do with the message received according to 1 Corinthians 15:2?

3. Summarize the message that was handed on from 1 Corinthians 15:3-7?

4. When did Jesus appear to Paul, according to 1 Corinthians 15:8?

5. What details of this appearance are recorded in Acts 9:3-6, 17-19?

6. Why does Paul call himself "unfit" to be an apostle?
   1 Corinthians 15:9
   Acts 8:3

7. What does Paul credit for the work he does now in 1 Corinthians 15:10?

8. What was the result of the apostles' proclaiming in 1 Corinthians 15:11?

COME TO ME

Reflection

1. Who shared the good news with you?

2. This reading says the Corinthians "received the good news and stood firm in it." How has there been a growing or progressing in your faith that would be a fruit of having received and stood firm? Explain.

3. The following quote is taken from Pope Paul VI.[41]
"Those who sincerely accept the good news...gather together in Jesus' name in order to seek together the kingdom and build it up and live it. They make up a community which is in its turn evangelizing....Those who have received the good news and who have been gathered by it into the community of salvation can and must communicate and spread it....Thus it is the whole Church that receives the mission to evangelize, and the work of each individual member is important for the whole."
When you accept the good news of Jesus Christ, why do you think this would call you to gather as community and proclaim this good news to others? How do you do this?

4. If a friend or interested person were to ask you to explain your faith, how would you present a summary of the gospel?

Closing Prayer

God our Father, by your grace we are your children. May we proclaim to all your goodness, your steadfast love, and your faithfulness. Continue to strengthen us to build your kingdom. Amen.

CHAPTER 27

Sixth Sunday of Ordinary Time Year C

Opening Song
Opening Prayer

Open in prayer and invite everyone to add their own prayer. Close together: "Jesus, I trust in you. Amen."

Review Study Guidelines

First Reading   Jeremiah 17:5-8

Setting the Stage

The first reading is from the book of the prophet Jeremiah. Jeremiah lives about 600 years before Jesus, and more than any other prophet he shares his spiritual struggle with God our Father.[42] Jeremiah is criticizing Judah for unfaithfulness in the practice of their faith. Through these words, and also in the words of the psalm that follows, God our Father gives us a comparison between those who put their trust in Him and those who put their trust elsewhere, and he shows us the consequences.

Read the first reading aloud. Reread this Scripture.
What word, phrase, or idea stands out for you?

Exploring Further

    1. Who is cursed according to Jeremiah 17:5?

2. What results when we trust in humans as described in Jeremiah 17:6?

3. Who is blessed, according to Jeremiah 17:7?

4. How is the person who trusts in the Lord described and how are they sustained in hard times?
   Jeremiah 17:8
   Psalm 1

5. How might Jesus' words be life giving during hard times, according to Luke 6:20-23, Sunday's gospel?

Reflection

1. At this time in your life do you feel like a bush in the desert, a tree by the river, other?

2. Consider the following comments.
   "I find that in most cases tension and anxiety arise when I am inwardly attached to something; my opinions, my plan, my desires, my wants, my needs, etc. I've also found that the harder I cling to whatever I'm holding onto, the more my anxiety levels rise. I believe that tension and anxiety point out to us our need to let go and trust the Lord. When we trust and learn inner detachment we become more and more free. This interior freedom is not dependent on circumstances. It is the fruit of a trusting heart."[43]
   - Can you relate to increasing anxiety as you cling to your ways, desires, plans, etc.? Explain. Do you think this indicates a need to let go and trust God? Why or why not?
   - How can we become more detached to our ways? What is causing you anxiety at this point? What do you need to let go of?

3. During the Second World War, the Lord told St. Faustina to teach others this prayer, "Jesus, I trust in you." During times of "heat" and "drought" in your life, how might this prayer be helpful to you? Is it easy or hard for you to trust? Explain.

4. From past experience, what has been a vessel for God's living water to sustain you?

Optional Exercise before the second reading. Have each person in the group briefly tell something of their past week or of an event anticipated in the coming week. This could be a time to share a triumph, a trial, or a need.

Sixth Sunday of Ordinary Time Year C

Second Reading 1 Corinthians 15:12, 16-20

Setting the Stage

The next reading is from the first letter that St. Paul wrote to the church in Corinth, Greece. Many Greeks at this time think the human body has no place after death.[44] In response St. Paul points out the implications of that error. The question being addressed is: *how do we know our bodies will rise again?*

Read this reading aloud. Reread this Scripture.
What word, phrase, or idea stands out for you?

Exploring Further

1. What two opposing beliefs are present among the Corinthians in 1 Corinthians 15:12?

2. If Christ is not raised, where does that leave us according to 1 Corinthians 15:16-18?

3. What is the good news in 1 Corinthians 15:20?

4. If our hope is for this life only, what is the result in 1 Corinthians 15:19?

5. What is now and what is to come according to Luke 6:20-26, Sunday's gospel?

6. What is made clear in Romans 8:11?

7. What will happen at the end of time according to 1 Thessalonians 4:14, 16?

Reflection

1. If our faith is only for this life, why would we be pitiable?

2. When we celebrate Christ's victory over death and his resurrection, we also celebrate our victory over death and our resurrection. What does this mean to you? Does this give you hope and courage? Why or why not?

3. In the Corinthian community two opposing beliefs were held. In your community today, how do you respond when opposing beliefs are presented?

Closing Prayer

Lord, our hope is in you. Cleanse and renew us, and lead us to our eternal reward. Amen.

CHAPTER 28
SEVENTH SUNDAY OF ORDINARY TIME YEAR C

OPENING SONG
OPENING PRAYER

Open in prayer and invite everyone to add their own prayer. Close together: "The Lord is kind and merciful. Amen."

REVIEW STUDY GUIDELINES

First Reading   1 Samuel 26:2, 7-9, 12-13, 22-25

Setting the Stage

This reading is from the first book of Samuel. We hear of an event in the life of David, who is to succeed King Saul as king of the Israelites in 1,000 BC. Saul has become jealous of the popularity of David and sets out in pursuit of him in the area of Ziph, 25 miles west of the southern tip of the Dead Sea. To our world of violence, where retaliation is a common policy, *God our Father presents this striking example of David.*

Read the first reading aloud. Reread this Scripture.
What word, phrase, or idea stands out for you?

Exploring Further

1. Where is Saul situated in the camp and how secure does he appear to be according to 1 Samuel 26:5?

Come to Me

2. What do David and Abishai do in 1 Samuel 26:7?

3. How does Abishai view the situation and what does he think should be done to Saul in 1 Samuel 26:8?

4. Saul had been trying to kill David. What do we discover about revenge in Romans 12:19?

5. How does David respond in 1 Samuel 26:9?

6. What is David willing to leave up to God in 1 Samuel 26:10?

7. How do David's actions line up to the words of Jesus in Luke 6:27-31, Sunday's gospel?

8. What does David take as proof of being close to Saul in 1 Samuel 26:12a?

9. What divine help does David receive according to 1 Samuel 26:12b?

10. What happens when God causes a deep sleep to fall in the following verses?
    Genesis 2:21-22
    Genesis 15:12-14

11. What does Saul acknowledge in 1 Samuel 26:21?

12. What does David do with the king's spear in 1 Samuel 26:22?

13. What does David say the Lord rewards in 1 Samuel 26:23?

14. What hope does David express in 1 Samuel 26:24?

15. How do the words of Jesus confirm David's hope in Luke 6:35-38?

Reflection

1. David respected Saul's position as king, even though David was treated unfairly. Consider positions of authority in our day; political leaders, ministers, teachers, parents, police, etc. Do you think the people in these positions should be shown respect, despite how they may sometimes act? Why or why not.

2. Have you ever been mistreated by someone in authority and if so how did you respond? When authority is misused, how do seeking justice and seeking revenge differ?

Seventh Sunday of Ordinary Time Year C

3. David respected Saul's life and was willing to let God be in control of when and how Saul was to die. What results when respect for life is absent? How can you show respect for life toward the disabled, elderly, the marginalized, those with terminal illnesses, etc. and let God be God of life and death? How does the church apply the sanctity of life principle and mercy to capital punishment?

4. David was merciful to Saul who was trying to kill him. Jesus said to love your enemies, do good to those who hate you, be merciful, and do not condemn. In what situation in your life can you put this into practice? If unable to do this, what stops you?

Optional Exercise before the second reading. Have each person in the group briefly tell something of their past week or of an event anticipated in the coming week. This could be a time to share a triumph, a trial, or a need.

Second Reading   1 Corinthians 15:45-50

Setting the Stage

The next reading is from the first letter St. Paul writes to the church in Corinth, Greece, about the year 55 AD. "Greeks have no trouble in conceiving the immortality of the soul, but the idea of a raised body is difficult."⁴⁵ St. Paul compares Adam (written of in the book of Genesis) with Jesus who is called "the last Adam." Through these words, God our Father is telling us *which one of them gives us life that lasts forever.*

Read the second reading aloud. Reread this Scripture.
What word, phrase, or idea stands out for you?

Exploring Further

1. What comparison is made between Adam and Christ in 1 Corinthians 15:45-47?

2. How does Adam come to be according to Genesis 2:7, and what gives him life?

3. How does Jesus become man according to Luke 1:35?

4. What comparison is made between Adam and Christ in 1 Corinthians 15:20-21?

5. What is truth about all people according to 1 Corinthians 15:48-50?

6. Since all are born of Adam, how can we inherit the kingdom?
   1 Corinthians 15:51-53
   John 3:3-7
   Philippians 3:20-21

7. What hope do the following Scriptures give you?
   Romans 6:4
   Romans 8:11
   Ephesians 2:4-6

8. What glimpse of the glorified body do we get from the following Scriptures?
   John 20:11-17a
   John 20:19-20

Reflection

1. These Scriptures show how the flesh and the physical body cannot enter heaven; only the spirit, the imperishable, and the spiritual body can enter heaven. Since all are born of flesh, how do you understand the change that needs to take place in order to enter heaven?

2. Do you struggle with the concept of the resurrection of the body? Explain. How do you understand the idea that our physical bodies will be raised, yet no longer be flesh or perishable?

3. Our resurrected bodies will no longer suffer, be handicapped, or give us pain. How might we apply this truth to help in times of suffering? One of the most difficult things in life is to watch a loved one suffer. Why would allowing God to be God of life and death be important at this time? How might God use this suffering for good in both the loved one and his family and friends?

Closing Prayer

Thanks be to God, who gives us the victory through our Lord Jesus Christ. Amen (1 Cor. 15: 57).

Eighth Sunday of Ordinary Year C

Opening Song
Opening Prayer

Open in prayer and invite everyone to add their own prayer. Close together: "Lord, search me and purify my heart that I may sing of your goodness and glorify your name. Amen."

Review Study Guidelines

First Reading   Sirach 27:4-7 (See appendix one.)

Setting the Stage

The first reading is from the book of Sirach, also called Ecclesiasticus. This book of wise sayings is written about 180 years before Jesus. In this short reading God our Father talks to us about the use of our tongues. *What happens when we speak?*

Read the first reading aloud. Reread this Scripture.
What word, phrase, or idea stands out for you?

Exploring Further

1. What sifts our virtue and our faults according to Sirach 27:4?

Come to Me

What does conversation test and what is this testing compared with in Sirach 27:5?

3. What will fire purify in the following Scriptures?
   Malachi 3:2-3
   1 Corinthians 3:11-15

4. What does the fruit of speech reveal according to Sirach 27:6?

5. What do our words and actions reveal according to Luke 6:39-42, Sunday's gospel?

6. What does Jesus say about fruit? Where is our fruit or treasure stored? And how is this treasure or fruit brought forth according to Luke 6:43-45, Sunday's gospel?

7. What warnings regarding speech are given in the following Scriptures?
   Proverbs 6:16-19
   Proverbs 18:2
   Jeremiah 9:8
   James 1:26
   James 3:3-10

8. How is speech a blessing?
   Proverbs 10:19-21
   Proverbs 12:6
   Proverbs 15:1-2, 4

9. How should we use our speech?
   Psalm 16:7
   Psalm 35:28
   Psalm 37:30-31
   Psalm 119:171-172
   Romans 10:8-10
   Hebrews 13:15

10. What advice is given in Sirach 27:7?

Reflection

1. What have you learned about yourself by hearing something you spoke?

2. How do you rate the control you have over your tongue or speech? In what ways can the tongue do damage? How can the tongue bring life and healing?

Eighth Sunday of Ordinary Time Year C

3. In the above Scriptures we are encouraged to use our tongues to praise God, to speak of the righteousness of God, to speak wisdom, to confess Jesus as Lord, to sing, and to offer a sacrifice of praise. Is this form of speech a regular part of your day? Explain. How can you increase this type of speech in your life?

4. Jesus tells us that what we speak comes forth from what is in our hearts. What can we do to ensure good fruit in our speech?

Optional Exercise before the second reading. Have each person in the group briefly tell something of their past week or of an event anticipated in the coming week. This could be a time to share a triumph, a trial, or a need.

Second Reading   1 Corinthians 15:54-58

Setting the Stage

The next reading is from the first letter of St. Paul to the church in Corinth, Greece. For many Greeks the idea of a risen and imperishable body after death is hard to understand. St. Paul quotes two Old Testament texts, from Isaiah and Hosea. In this reading, God our Father is showing us *who is more powerful than sin* and more powerful than the Jewish Law, in transforming and giving life to our human bodies.

Read aloud. Reread this Scripture.
What word, phrase, or idea stands out for you?

Exploring Further

1. What will happen to our bodies according to 1 Corinthians 15:51-55?

2. What is promised or foretold by the prophets?
    Isaiah 25:8
    Hosea 13:14

3. What is said about sin in 1 Corinthians 15:56?

5. How does the Law give sin power?
    Romans 3:19-20
    Romans 4:13-15

Come to Me

      Romans 5:13
      Romans 7:7-10, 12
      Galatians 3:10

6. How do we gain victory over sin?
    1 Corinthians 15:57
    Romans 5:8-11
    Romans 10:4
    Galatians 3:22-27
    Matthew 5:17

7. What law do we now live under?
    John 13:34
    Romans 13:8-10
    Galatians 6:2

8. Since we have victory over sin and death through faith in Jesus, how should we live?
    1 Corinthians 15:58
    John 16:33
    Philippians 2:14-16

Reflection

1. The law gives us information about right and wrong and makes us conscious of sin but does not give us the strength to do what is right. How does knowledge of the law increase fault when we fail to keep the law? How have you experienced a struggle between knowing what is right and doing what is right?

2. Jesus perfectly fulfills the law and we can become righteous through faith and baptism in Jesus. We are now called to love one another as Jesus loved us. Jesus and the power of the Holy Spirit and the mercy of forgiveness make it possible. As believers, there is still an expectation in how we live and act. What is different between living under the old law and living as believers in Jesus? What is the same in struggling to do right and what is different?

3. How does your faith make you steadfast and immoveable? How are you laboring for the work of the Lord? What gives you hope to continue?

Closing Prayer

Father, we thank you for giving us victory through your Son, Jesus Christ. May we shine like bright stars as we labor to bring the world the Word of Life. Amen.

CHAPTER 30

NINTH SUNDAY OF ORDINARY TIME YEAR C

OPENING SONG
OPENING PRAYER

Open in prayer and invite everyone to add their own prayer. Close together: "Lord, may we live what we believe that all people will desire to seek and learn from the Living God. Amen."

REVIEW STUDY GUIDELINES

First Reading   1 Kings 8:42-43

Setting the Stage

The first reading is from the first book of Kings which shows King Solomon praying after the completion of the first Temple built in Jerusalem about 1, 000 years before Jesus. Through these words God our Father tells us whose prayers will be heard in his Temple. *Will a person's nationality count?*

Read the first reading aloud. Reread this Scripture.
What word, phrase, or idea stands out for you?

Exploring Further

1. Why would a foreigner come to Israel according to 1 Kings 8:41-42?

2. What does Solomon ask of God and why, in 1 Kings 8:43?

3. What is foretold in the following Scriptures?
   Isaiah 2:2-3
   Jeremiah 16:19-21
   Zechariah 8:20-23

4. It is foretold that people from every nation will seek the Lord and his teaching. What is Jesus' plan for making this happen in Matthew 28:19-20?

5. What prompts two foreigners to seek the Lord and what are the results?
   Luke 7:1-10, Sunday's gospel
   Acts 8:26-39

6. How are the Hebrews treated when they are foreigners?
   Exodus1:12-14, 16
   Exodus 2:23

7. How does God say the foreigner should be treated?
   Leviticus 23:22
   Deuteronomy 26:12

8. What does God remind the Israelites of in Exodus 22:21?

Reflection

1. Keeping in mind that circumcision prefigures baptism, why do you think the foreigners were required to be circumcised before participating in the Passover? Why is baptism necessary before participating in the Eucharist?

2. In the readings today it is foretold that many will seek the Lord because of his mighty deeds and great name, desire the Lord to teach them that they may walk in his paths, and revere his name and walk in the light of the Lord. Which of these is a desire of your heart? Explain. When seeking the Lord, the centurion received healing for his servant and the Ethiopian learned of the risen Lord. What motivated you to seek the Lord? What has resulted so far from this seeking?

3. How can believers be a part of proclaiming the mighty deeds of the Lord, teaching his ways and being an example of walking in his paths? How can we be a hindrance?

4. In today's readings the people were told to leave some of the harvest that the poor and foreigner could gather food [provide work], to help the poor and foreigner that they may continue to live in their midst [assist with aid and support], and to give a portion of their tithe to them [giving money

to the poor and foreigner]. How many generations ago were your family immigrants? What help did they receive? How generous is our country in allowing immigrants to come here and assisting immigrants to live among us?

Optional Exercise before the second reading. Have each person in the group briefly tell something of their past week or of an event anticipated in the coming week. This could be a time to share a triumph, a trial, or a need.

Second Reading — Galatians 1:1-2, 6-10

Setting the Stage

The second reading is from St. Paul's letter written about 25 years after the resurrection of Jesus to the Christians in Galatia which is now known as central Turkey. There is a big problem here. Some preachers have come to these people after Paul has left and are saying that Paul's preaching is wrong. These new preachers say that all converts have to follow the Jewish law and customs. We hear Paul's angry response, and he gives his credentials as an apostle. The question that is being addressed is: *from whom do true preachers get their authority so that we can trust them?*

Read the second reading aloud. Reread this Scripture.
What word, phrase, or idea stands out for you?

Exploring Further

1. How does Paul identify himself and who gave him his mission in Galatians 1:1-2?

2. How is Paul commissioned?
   Galatians 1:11-16
   Acts 26:12-18

3. The Galatians are combining Jewish faith practices as necessary for salvation along with their faith in Jesus Christ. How does Paul view this practice Galatians 1:6-9?

4. What does faith look like in Luke 7:6-9, Sunday's gospel?

5. What results when we believe the good news?
   Acts 15:8-11
   Acts 16:30-34
   Ephesians 1:13-14

6. What are we to remember and do when presented with opposing spiritual ideas?
   John 8:31-32
   1 Corinthians 15:1-5
   2 Thessalonians 2:14-15
   Hebrews 4:14-16

7. What is Paul's first priority?
   Galatians 1:10
   1 Thessalonians 2:2-4

Reflection

1. Salvation comes from God through faith in Jesus Christ. Faith is a personal response to God's initiative. Faith is then lived out as a people, nurtured and supported by the church, and grows to maturity by spiritual practices and service. Just as some Jews in today's reading mistakenly thought Jewish practices were necessary for salvation, how can Christians at times believe spiritual practices and service or "being good" are the means of salvation?

2. Today, traditional Christian values are seldom lived out in our society. The spirituality of many non-Christian religions is popular. How do we balance learning, being open to others, and recognizing truth in unexpected places with staying firmly rooted in the truths and traditions of faith as handed on by Jesus and the disciples?

3. Paul is most concerned about pleasing God. When do the pressures of pleasing others or yourself make it hard to do what is pleasing to God?

Closing Prayer

Lord, gives us the strength and courage to finish the race, standing firm in faith with our eyes fixed on Jesus. Amen.

SECTION FOUR

LENT

Lent is a period of forty days of preparation and does not include Sundays, which are always celebrated as "mini-Easters."

In the time of Noah it rained for forty days and forty nights, destroying the old and preparing Noah for a new life. Moses and the Israelites spent forty years in the desert learning to know and trust God their redeemer. Jesus spent forty days in the desert totally trusting God in preparation for his ministry.

The traditional hallmarks of Lent are prayer, fasting and almsgiving.

Jesus' time of prayer in the desert before embarking on his ministry is intense. What does this say to you about your need to set aside a time for more intense prayer? Lent is such a time.

Jesus' fasts in the desert makes him weak and vulnerable. In doing so he experiences strength by trusting God. By emptying himself Jesus is able to be filled with the spirit and power of God. Self-reliance prevents God-reliance. What do you need to fast from in order to be vulnerable and to rely on God? Is your life so full that there is no room for God or the things of God? Where do you need to empty your life to make room for God? What do you need to fast from in order to be able to receive from God?

We are called to give alms, to be aware of those in need and to help them. We need to be generous as God is generous to us. When we give generously of ourselves, we deepen our trust in God's care and providence for us.

"Is this not the fast that I choose: to loose the bonds of injustice, to undo the thongs of the yoke, to let the oppressed go free, and to break every yoke? Is it not to share your bread with the hungry, and bring the homeless poor into your house; when you see the naked, to cover them, and not to hide yourself from your own kin?"

—Isaiah 58:6-7

Prayer, fasting and almsgiving are always connected with justice. As we seek a deeper relationship with Jesus, we will be led to seek just relationships with and for others.

Lord, help me to use these forty days of Lent to let go of the old and open to the new life you have for me. Help me to become empty and vulnerable so that I may be filled with you. Teach me to trust you and to give generously of my time, resources, and talents just as you give so generously to me. Lord, show me where my life contributes to injustice for others and give me the courage to change. Help me use these forty days wisely. Amen.

*Here is the Lamb of God
who takes away the sin of the world!*

(John 1:29)

A cross created by nature in the rock face on Roche Miette,
Jasper Nation Park, Alberta, Canada.

CHAPTER 31

First Sunday of Lent Year C

Opening Song
Opening Prayer

Open in prayer and invite everyone to add their own prayer. Close together: "Lord, you deliver those who love you. You protect those who call to you. When we call, you answer, you rescue us from trouble, and you honor us. What a mighty God we have. Amen."

Review Study Guidelines

First Reading   Deuteronomy 26:4-10

Setting the Stage

All Lenten readings are meant to prepare us for Easter. The first readings from the Old Testament are like predictions of what we celebrate at Easter, that is, our passage from sin and death to life! The second readings show how we take part in the death and resurrection of Jesus. The gospel readings present stories from the earthly ministry of Jesus. This first reading today is from the book of Deuteronomy. We see Moses speaking to God's people about the custom of offering "first fruits," that is, offering a sample of the things that first ripen in their gardens and fields. Notice their "creed," what they believed about their history, what God our Father has done for them. The expression "My father is a wandering Aramean" refers to Jacob, the grandson of Abraham. Jacob has emigrated from Palestine to Egypt with his family about 1700 BC.

The questions being addressed are: Who are the people of that day supposed to worship, and how? Who are we to worship, and is our creed similar?

Come to Me

Read the first reading aloud. Reread this Scripture.
What word, phrase, or idea stands out for you?

Exploring Further

1. In this liturgical ceremony, what are the people bringing in Deuteronomy 26:2?

2. What should the value of this offering be according to Exodus 23:19?

3. Deuteronomy 26:5-9 is the creed or belief in what God has done for them that the people verbalize while presenting their offering at the altar. How is Jacob described and what happens while the Israelites live in Egypt in Deuteronomy 25:5?

4. Why is their growing number seen as a problem according to Exodus 1:8-12?

5. How are the Israelites treated by the Egyptians according to Deuteronomy 26:6?

6. How is the hard labor of the Israelites described in Exodus 1:13-14?

7. In their misery, what do the people do according to Deuteronomy 26:7?

8. What hardships and temptations does Jesus suffer and what is his response in each case in Sunday's gospel?
   Luke 4:1-4
   Luke 4:5-8
   Luke 4: 9-13

9. How does God respond to their affliction according to Deuteronomy 26:8?

10. What two actions do the people take to show gratitude for God's goodness to them in Deuteronomy 26:10?

Reflection

1. In Deuteronomy, the people professed their belief, presented their offering, and worshipped God. Consider our Sunday worship:
   – What creed do we profess?
   – What gift do we offer? Do you give a "choice" gift? Explain.
   – How do we bow before God or worship?

2. In your opinion, would someone observing your weekly participation and attitude in professing your belief, offering your gift, and your worship conclude you are a grateful believing person? Why or why not?

3. Is regularly professing our belief, giving a choice gift, and worship a just and reasonable response for what God has done for us? Why or why not?

4. Our spiritual journey is lived at both a community level and an individual level. Take a few minutes for everyone to answer the following questions and then break up into pairs and share with one other person your personal creed:
   - Where were you or what affliction or oppression did you experience that caused you to call out to God?
   - How did God respond when you called out?
   - Where did God lead you? (Or whom did God put in your life?)
   - What gift of your life and talents have you since been able to offer to God?
   - How has your experience caused you to bow before God and in what ways have you learned to worship God?

Optional Exercise before the second reading. Have each person in the group briefly tell something of their past week or of an event anticipated in the coming week. This could be a time to share a triumph, a trial, or a need.

Second Reading   Romans 10:8-13

Setting the Stage

The second reading is from the letter of St. Paul written in the winter of 57-58 AD to the church in Rome. Paul is inspired by God our Father to write about the choice that people of every nationality have—of either trusting in Jesus[46] or not. He gives the Scripture quotations from the book of Deuteronomy and the prophet Joel.

The question being addressed is: *Is Jesus far away or…?*

Read this reading aloud. Reread this Scripture.
What word, phrase, or idea stands out for you?

COME TO ME

Exploring Further

1. Where does the Word of faith reside according to Romans 10:8?

2. This statement by Paul is a quote from Deuteronomy. What does this say about the accessibility of the word and what it calls us to in Deuteronomy 30:11-14.?

3. How does Jesus deal with Satan's temptations in Luke 4:4, 8, 12?

4. What are we to confess and believe according to Romans 10:9?

5. What is the result of this confession?

6. How is this reiterated in Romans 10:10?

7. What is promised in Acts 16:31 when we believe?

8. Abraham is an example to us of someone who believed. What does Romans 4:20-25 say regarding how he grew in faith, what his faith resulted in, and how this applies to us too?

9. What promise is given in Romans 10:11?

10. What does Romans 10:12 say regarding the availability of salvation for all?

11. What must everyone do according to Romans 10:13?

12. How do we receive faith according to Romans 10:17?

13. What responsibility are we called to in Romans 10:14-15?

Reflection

1. Have you ever acknowledged from your heart and with your mouth that Jesus is Lord or made a conscious decision to say "yes" to your baptismal promise? Explain.

2. Have other people shared their faith in Jesus with you? What difference did it make?
Have you ever had a bad experience when talking to someone about Jesus? Explain. What do you think should be avoided when proclaiming Jesus?

3. Have you ever shared your faith in Jesus with someone else? Explain. If not, what prevents you from talking to others about Jesus?

Closing Prayer

Father, increase our faith and hope and deepen our love. We believe that Jesus is Lord. Amen.

CHAPTER 32

Second Sunday of Lent Year C

Opening Song
Opening Prayer

Open in prayer and invite everyone to add their own prayer. Close together: "Faith is being sure of what we hope for and certain of what we do not see. Lord, I believe you will do what you have promised. Amen."

Review Study Guidelines

First Reading   Genesis 15: 5-12, 17-18

Setting the Stage

The first reading is from the book of Genesis. It is about an event in the life of Abraham who lives about 1800 BC. Originally his name is "Abram," and his family roots are in Ur, a city of the Chaldeans (Babylonians) located on the Euphrates River, 150 miles inland from the Persian Gulf in what is now Iraq. Abraham travels west to Palestine through Haran (southern Turkey). God tells him that he will be the founding father of a family more numerous than the stars. This great family is to include all the Jews and all the Christians of history. But Abraham at the time does not even have one son, and he is already a very old man. He wonders how this could possibly come to be, so *he asks God for a sign* that this promise will come true. The sign is very strange to us moderns, but it is the ancient way of making a contract or agreement. An animal is cut in two halves and the people making the deal will both walk between the halves. This means that if either one breaks the contract then they will be cut in half too. Birds are not cut as they were too small. The agreement God makes with Abraham is called a "covenant." Note the following:

1. In the Old Testament, God our Father is very often symbolized by fire; and in this reading we hear of a "smoking fire pot" and a "flaming torch."
2. Notice also who is the only one who walks between the halves!
3. The vultures, "birds of prey," symbolize the dangers that will threaten the covenant.
4. Notice all the elements of a supernatural happening, a "theophany"—the setting sun, the deep sleep, fear, and darkness. *When God gives us a sign, what does that mean?*

Read the first reading aloud. Reread this Scripture.
What word, phrase, or idea stands out for you?

Exploring Further

1. What concern does Abram express in Genesis 15:2?

2. What is God's response that gives Abram a glimpse of what is to come in Genesis 15:5?

3. How does Abram respond to God's promise in Genesis 15:6a?

4. How does Abram's response count to the Lord in Genesis 15:6b?

5. What is the result of Abraham's faith according to Galatians 3:6-9?

6. What promise do we have in Romans 10:9-10? Do you believe this?

7. List what Abraham does by faith as summarized in Hebrews 11:8-12?

8. What does God do to further assure Abram of his promise in Genesis 17:1-5?

9. What does God promise Abram and what is Abram's response in Genesis 15:7-8?

10. What is God's answer to Abram in Genesis 15:9-12, 17-18?

11. What glimpse of glory and confirmation do Peter, James, and John witness in Luke 9:28, 35-36, Sunday's gospel?

12. With help from "Setting the Stage" and today's reading, answer the following:
    How is the covenant made and what does it symbolize?
    What do the birds of prey symbolize?

Second Sunday of Lent Year C

How is God pictured as walking between the animals?

Only God passed between the halves. What might this say about God?

13. How does Abram deal with the birds of prey in Genesis 15:11?

Reflection

1. Consider the many promises of God to us in Scripture, and possible ones you have been given personally. What promises from God are most meaningful to you today? Explain.

2. After God makes Abram a promise about possessing the land he cries out "Lord God, how can I know?" We too may cry out "Lord God, how can I know?" during times of bereavement, unemployment, when loved ones seem to have wandered far from God, in loneliness, or in abusive situations. How have you experienced God in hard times?

3. Just as God made a covenant with Abraham, he also made a covenant with us by the sacrifice of Jesus on the cross. The sign of this covenant is Eucharist. Does this covenant give you hope during hard times? Explain.

4. What "birds of prey" can attack our faith journey? How can we drive away these attacks?

Optional Exercise before the second reading. Have each person in the group briefly tell something of their past week or of an event anticipated in the coming week. This could be a time to share a triumph, a trial, or a need.

Second Reading Philippians 3:17–4:1

Setting the Stage

The second reading is from the letter St. Paul writes to the church in Philippi, located in northern Greece, when he is in a prison in southwestern Turkey about 57 AD. He had set up this church in the year 50 and the people there are his good friends. So when they hear that St. Paul is in prison, they send him help. St. Paul writes this letter back to thank them. He also wants to encourage them in their faith because there are some Jewish-Christian preachers at Philippi who are saying that Christians have to do what Jews have always done—follow special food laws (abstain from pork, etc.) and males are to be circumcised. The question being addressed here is: *what is more important—following food laws or sharing with the poor? And what does Easter tell us about the destiny of our human body?*

Read the second reading aloud. Reread this Scripture. What word, phrase, or idea stands out for you?

Exploring Further

1. What advice is given in Philippians 3:17?

2. What warning is given in the following Scriptures?
   Philippians 3:18-19
   Romans 16:18

3. Where is our citizenship according to Philippians 3:20?

4. What is the attitude of those who have gone before us in faith in Hebrews 11:13-16?

5. When Jesus returns, what will he do according to Philippians 3:21?

6. During our struggles here on earth, what hope and glimpse of glory are given?
   Colossians 3:1-4
   Romans 8:23
   1 John 3:2

7. What vision of divine glory are Peter, John, and James given in Luke 9:28-31, Sunday's gospel?

8. How do the apostles almost miss this moment of glory in Luke 9:32?

9. What does Paul urge in Philippians 4:1?

10. Paul refers to his brothers and sisters as his joy and crown. In 1 Thessalonians 2:19-20, what seems to be the reward for sharing our faith in Jesus with others?

Reflection

1. We are encouraged to imitate those who lead godly lives. Who are people that have affected your life that you try to imitate? How can studying the lives of the saints help us?

2. What are practical ways we can live with our eyes on things above, remembering that heaven is our true home?

Second Sunday of Lent Year C

3. Consider the following reflection:

Visions of glory help us to trust [as did Abraham's vision in the first reading and the disciple's vision in Luke]. But all glory, even the glory of creation, comes from sacrifice: stars and suns are born from violent deaths of earlier stars, saplings take root in decayed stumps and become great firs. [47] Pine cones burst forth after a forest fire, birth follows labor pains, Jesus' resurrection and glory followed suffering and death, and martyrs' blood is the seedbed of faith.

If glory follows sacrifice, what situation in your life can you possibly look at in a new way? Is there an area in your life that you need to sacrifice or die to so new life can grow? Explain.

Closing Prayer

God our Father help us to hear your son. Enlighten us with your Word, that we may find the way to your glory. Amen.

CHAPTER 33

THIRD SUNDAY OF LENT
YEAR C

Note: For parishes engaged in the RCIA, this Sunday is the first scrutiny. The readings from the third Sunday of Lent year C-A, "Come and Drink", will be read.

OPENING SONG

OPENING PRAYER

Open in prayer and invite everyone to add their own prayer. Close together: "Lord, you have observed our suffering and misery. Lead us out of bondage and into new life we pray. Amen."

REVIEW STUDY GUIDELINES

First Reading   Exodus 3:1-8a, 13-15

Setting the Stage

The first reading is from the book of Exodus, which tells us how God's people escape from slavery in Egypt to find freedom in Palestine, the Promised Land. Today's reading shows us a very important moment in the life of Moses. This takes place around 1300 BC. Moses has escaped from Egypt and is living near Mount Sinai, also known as Horeb. This mountain is located at the tip of the Sinai Peninsula where the Midianite people live. Note: 1. "The angel of the Lord" signifies God our Father himself (fire signifies divine presence); 2. "I Am who I Am" and "I Am" are the English translations of the Hebrew word "YAHWEH."

Read the first reading aloud. Reread this Scripture.
What word, phrase, or idea stands out for you?

Come to Me

Exploring Further

1. What is Moses doing and how is this a foreshadowing and preparation for his future role with God's people in Exodus 3:1?

2. Where is Moses?

3. Why is Horeb considered the mountain of God?
   Deuteronomy 5:2-4
   Malachi 4:4

4. How does God attract Moses' attention in Exodus 3:2-3?

5. How does God call Moses and how does Moses respond in Exodus 3:4b?

6. What might doubling a name signify?
   Genesis 22:11
   1 Samuel 3:1

7. What directions are given in Exodus 3:5?

8. What does the setting of boundaries in approaching God signify?
   Exodus 19:12, 21-24
   Numbers 1:52
   Numbers 18:22

Note: Transcendence and holiness are inseparable and holiness implies separation from the profane. Where God manifests his presence is forbidden ground. For the same reason the ark must not be handled. This idea of the sacred, though primitive, conveys a lesson of enduring worth: that the mystery of God's greatness is impenetrable and his majesty a thing of awe.[48]

9. Have these boundaries changed and if so, how?
   Matthew 27:50-51
   Hebrews 10:19-23

10. How does God identify himself in Exodus 3:6?

11. Why would Moses be afraid to look at God?
    Exodus 33:19-20
    Exodus 2:11-15

Third Sunday of Lent Year C

12. What has the Lord observed and what does he plan to do in Exodus 3:7-8?

13. What mission does God give Moses in Exodus 3:10?

14. What does God say his name is in Exodus 3:14-15?

Note: God reminded Moses of the covenant promises to Abraham, Isaac, and Jacob and used the name *I Am* to show his unchanging nature. What God promised to the great patriarchs hundreds of years earlier he would now fulfill through Moses.[49]

15. What results from knowing God's name according to Psalm 9:10?

Reflection

1. God called Moses by name and revealed himself to Moses. This is conversion, a place of knowing—a God experience. Have you had a similar experience? Explain.

2. After his "God experience," Moses was sent to God's people. Where and to whom have you been sent? Explain. Moses also had to go back and face his past. What areas in your life that were fearful or hidden has God taken you back to deal with? What difference has this made?

3. In Old Testament times, to enter the Holy of Holies, touch the Ark of the Covenant, or come too close to God in a sacred place meant death. This envoked reverence, awe, and fear. Through the blood of Jesus we are now able to approach God with confidence, as Abba, with intimacy. What do you think are appropriate ways and attitudes to approach God the Father? What are possible extremes that should be avoided?

Optional Exercise before the second reading. Have each person in the group briefly tell something of their past week or of an event anticipated in the coming week. This could be a time to share a triumph, a trial, or a need.

Second Reading   1 Corinthians 10:1-6, 10-12

Setting the Stage

The second reading is from the first letter that St. Paul writes to the church in Corinth, Greece, about 25 years after Jesus' resurrection. In this part of the letter St. Paul is responding to one of the problems the Corinthians are facing—taking God for granted. To make his point, he compares these Christians with the Hebrew people in their journey out of Egypt; they are led by a cloud, go through the Red Sea, and travel through the Sinai wilderness. St. Paul refers to an ancient legend of the Jewish rabbis—when the Hebrews are thirsty on their desert journey, God tells Moses to take his stick and hit a rock; when he does so, it becomes a spring of water. Later on, the rabbis teach that the rock rolled along behind the people so they will always have a source of fresh water. (Though the Old Testament says nothing about *the rock that followed* the Israelites in the wilderness, a later rabbinic tradition did say this about a well in Numbers 21:16-18.)[50] St. Paul makes that rock a symbol of a very important person. Who is this person? The question that is being addressed is: *do we take him for granted?*

Read the second reading aloud. Reread this Scripture.
What word, phrase, or idea stands out for you?

Exploring Further

1. What does Paul want the people to remember in 1 Corinthians 10:1?

2. What do the cloud and sea refer to?
   Exodus 13:21-22
   Exodus 14:22

3. What do the people do in common in 1 Corinthians 10:3-4?

4. What is the problem according to 1 Corinthians 10:5?

5. Read Exodus 16:4-30 and Numbers 11:4-6, 34; 20:7-13. Answer the following:
   What was the spiritual food given?
   What was the spiritual drink given?
   What is the rock Paul refers to?

Third Sunday of Lent Year C

> Why was God not pleased?
> What was the punishment?

6. What do the following Scriptures tell us about God?
   Hebrews 3:17-19
   Jude 5-7

7. What does Jesus say can be learned from the suffering of others in Luke 13:2-5, Sunday's gospel?

8. What should be avoided according to 1 Corinthians 10:10?

9. What is the purpose of recording the following events?
   1 Corinthians 10:11
   Romans 15:4

10. What encouragement is given in 1 Corinthians 10:13?

Reflection

1. We share in the same spiritual food and drink as our brothers and sisters in Christ. Do you think there are ways that God may not be pleased with us? Explain.

2. How have you taken God for granted?

3. What do you complain about? How is complaining destructive?

4. How is being grateful life-giving? How can we develop an attitude of gratitude?

5. What have you learned from your own mistakes or those of others?

6. God is merciful and loving. God punishes sin and disobedience. Why is it healthy to know both of these truths? Why do we have hope when we sin? What does this mean to you?

Closing Prayer:

Lord, you are merciful and just. We desire to be a grateful, obedient people. Amen.

CHAPTER 34

FOURTH SUNDAY OF LENT
YEAR C

Note: For a parish engaged in RCIA, this Sunday is the second scrutiny, and the fourth Sunday of Lent year C-A, "Come and Drink" will be used. Check with your parish.

OPENING SONG
OPENING PRAYER

Open in prayer and invite everyone to add their own prayer. Close together: "Lord, thank you for your goodness to us. Amen."

REVIEW STUDY GUIDELINES

First Reading   Joshua 5:9a, 10-12

Setting the Stage

The first reading is from the book of Joshua. Joshua is the right-hand man of Moses and becomes the leader of the Hebrew people when Moses dies. In today's reading we see them just after they enter the Promised Land of Israel—whose ancient name is Canaan. They have crossed to the west bank of the Jordan River near a town called Gigal, just north of Jericho. All this takes place about 1300 BC. *Passover* is the special Jewish feast commemorating all the things that happen during the escape from Egypt.

Read the first reading aloud. Reread this Scripture.
What word, phrase, or idea stands out for you?

COME TO ME

Exploring Further

1. What does God promise the Israelites in Joshua 5:9?

2. What is the disgrace referred to in Joshua 5:4-8?

3. What do the Israelites celebrate at Gilgal according to Joshua 5:10?

4. This is the first Passover in the Promised Land. The last Passover was celebrated at Mt. Sinai 39 years earlier. What did they celebrate then and always remember at every Passover following, according to Exodus 12:1-13, 17?

5. How does God provide for the Israelites according to Nehemiah 9:19-21?

6. Why is that no longer necessary according to Joshua 5:11-2?

Reflection

1. What do you think those people felt like after being "on the road" for 40 years?

2. What is your experience after a long, hard session is over? How did God provide for you during this time?

Optional Exercise before the second reading. Have each person in the group briefly tell something of their past week or of an event anticipated in the coming week. This could be a time to share a triumph, a trial, or a need.

Second Reading   2 Corinthians 5:12, 17-21

Setting the Stage

The next reading is from the first letter St. Paul writes to the church in Corinth, Greece. Some people have gone to Corinth after St. Paul established the church and said he is not a true apostle. This letter is a defense of his ongoing work as an apostle.

Fourth Sunday of Lent Year C

Read this reading aloud. Reread this Scripture.
What word, phrase, or idea stands out for you?

Exploring Further

1. What happens to one who is in Christ, according to 2 Corinthians 5:17?

2. What is Christ's role in creation from the beginning according to John 1:3?

3. After sin deformed the original creation, what does Christ say he will do?
   Colossians 1:15-20
   Ephesians 2:15
   Galatians 6:15
   2 Peter 3:13

4. How do we enter this new life according to Romans 6:4?

5. Who is this gift from and why, according to 2 Corinthians 5:19?

6. How is this role described in Ephesians 2:10?

7. What is God's work and what does he entrust to us in 2 Corinthians 5:19?

8. What does the son do to damage relationships with his family in Luke 15:12-13, Sunday's gospel?

9. How does the Father receive the repentant son in Luke 15:20-24?

10. How does the elder son receive his brother in Luke 10:25-30?

11. Who are we, according to 2 Corinthians 5:20a?

12. As ambassadors for Christ, what is the first thing we need to do according to 2 Corinthians 5:20b?

13. What foundational truth is mentioned in 2 Corinthians 5:21a?

14. What does Christ's sacrifice make us, according to 2 Corinthians 5:21b?

15. How are we declared righteous according to Philippians 3:9?

Come to Me

Reflection

1. Can you think of a time that someone trusted you? What happened? Can you think of a time that you trusted someone else? What happened?

2. Today's readings focus on reconciliation and forgiveness. How have you experienced reconciliation of a relationship? Are there relationships in your life not yet reconciled? Explain. Would you describe your relationship with God as feuding, a truce, or harmonious?

3. At Easter we shall renew our baptism, so it's important that we ask, "What happened to us in our baptism?"

4. Consider the following quote:

"Will it be as hard for the three-quarters of humanity—the developing world—to welcome us as it was for the elder son in the parable to celebrate the return of his prodigal brother? They have witnessed our profligate use of the world's resources. They have seen our wanton disregard for the global common good."[51]

- Can you see the first world countries as the younger son in the parable? Why or why not?
- What life-destroying choices do we need to turn away from in our use of the world's goods? How can we choose a lifestyle based on gospel values? Will we change only when we are forced to? Why do you think so?

Closing Prayer Examination of conscience.

Leader: *Thank you for removing our disgrace and delighting in us when we return to you. For the times we have not turned to you in repentance and held on to bitterness and resentment...*
Response: Father, forgive us.

Leader: *Thank you for the abundance of food and resources with which you have filled the earth. For the times we have not been good stewards in caring for and sharing this abundance...*
Response: Father, forgive us.

Leader: *Thank you for the gift of life. For the times we have squandered our life and gifts in dissolute living, selfishness and excess...*
Response: Father, forgive us.

Leader: *You called us to be ambassadors for Christ and ministers of reconciliation. For the times we have failed, as a church and individually, to be a witness to you and instead have caused hurt and division...*
Response: Father, forgive us.

Fourth Sunday of Lent Year C

Leader: *Thank you for your gift of mercy and compassion. For the times we have withheld been harsh to others or to ourselves...*
Response: Father, forgive us.

Leader: *Thank you for the gift of faith... For the times we neglected our faith life, neither praying nor nourishing it with the sacraments...*
Response: Father, forgive us.

Leader: *Father, you celebrate life. For the times we have refused to participate in life or have contributed to the culture of death by word or deed...*
Response: Father, forgive us.

All: Lord, all is gift, the faith to believe in your forgiveness and the forgiveness itself. We come to you with humility, to confess to you and to each other that we have sinned by abusing your gifts or by refusing them. We ask mercy, healing, and forgiveness. We ask you, Lord, to give us this day the wisdom and courage to begin anew. Lord, help us to be faithful in carrying your message of reconciliation to the world. Amen.

CHAPTER 35

Fifth Sunday of Lent Year C

Note For a parish engaged in RCIA, this Sunday is the third scrutiny and the fifth Sunday of Lent year C-A. There is a study in "Come and Drink" on these readings.

Opening Song

Opening Prayer

Open in prayer and invite everyone to add their own prayer. Close together: "Lord, we give praise and thanks that you have done great things for us. Amen."

Review Study Guidelines

First Reading   Isaiah 43:16-21

Setting the Stage

The first reading is from the book of the prophet Isaiah. These words are spoken about 540 years before Jesus. The Hebrew people have been deported to Babylonia (modern day Iraq). The big question is how would they ever get out of this difficulty? Who will help? The prophet reminds them of previous miracles done for their people 700 years earlier when they had to face the Red Sea on their escape from slavery in Egypt, and they are also reminded what happened to the Egyptian army in that sea. But for these Hebrews to get home from Babylonia, they will have to face the Syrian Desert. Will they be able to survive like the desert animals do? Through these words, God our Father tells *whom it is that we can depend on in our challenges.*

Come to Me

Read the first reading aloud. Reread this Scripture.
What word, phrase, or idea stands out for you?

Exploring Further

1. How is God described in Isaiah 43:15?

2. What does the Lord do according to Isaiah 43:16-17?

3. When did these events take place according to Exodus 14:21-24, 28-29?

4. Though mighty deeds were done in the past, what is to come according to Isaiah 43:18-19?

5. What do the following Scriptures say about the new things God is doing?
   Isaiah 65:17
   2 Corinthians 5:17
   Revelation 21:5

6. What speaks of God's life-giving care in Isaiah 43:20?

7. What previous experience do the people have of God providing water in the desert according to Exodus17:1-7?

8. Why will God have mercy on his chosen people and provide for them according to Isaiah 43:21?

9. Who are we and what are we called to do in 1 Peter 2:9-10?

10. What is the woman in Sunday's gospel able to praise God for and how does she experience God's mercies in John 8:1-11?

Reflection

1. Think of a time in your past when God helped you through a difficult time. What praise can you give him for what he did for you?

2. What "new thing" is God doing in your life today?

3. What "new thing" do you think God is doing in the church or world today?

Fifth Sunday of Lent Year C

Second Reading   Philippians 3:8-14

Setting the Stage

The next reading is from the letter of St. Paul to the church at Philippi, Greece. He has set up that church about the year 50 AD and made very close friends with the Christians; so much so that when he is put in prison for his faith about seven years later, they send a Christian to help Paul. He writes this letter to thank them and encourage them in their faith. Through St. Paul, God our Father is showing us the answer to this question: *What is more important, the Jewish religious law or faith in Jesus?*

Read this reading aloud. Reread this Scripture.
What word, phrase, or idea stands out for you?

Exploring Further

1. How does Paul regard his own accomplishments and what is his priority in Philippians 3:8?

2. What righteousness does Paul reject and what righteousness does he seek in Philippians 3:9?

3. What do you learn regarding righteousness in Romans 10:3?

4. What is Paul's desire in Philippians 3:10-11?

5. What do we learn about salvation and faith in the following?
   Romans 1:16
   Galatians 2:16

6. What is the outward sign of this faith?

7. What is Paul's single-minded goal according to Philippians 3:12-14?

8. What do the following Scriptures say about faithfulness in seeking Christ?
   Romans 2:6
   Galatians 5:7
   Luke 9:62
   1 Corinthians 9:25-27

Reflection

1. What are your priorities in life?

2. Have you suffered in any way or had to give up something in order to seek Christ and be found in him?

3. "Faith, which is the response of a human being to God as truth and goodness and so the one source of salvation, is reliance on the truth of God's promises and on God's faithfulness."[52] In light of this definition, what actions may demonstrate a reliance on our own righteousness? What actions demonstrate a reliance on the righteousness of God through faith?

4. If you compare your Christian journey with a race, which of the following would best describe you? a) Sprinting fast, b) pacing your run, c) injured, d) watching on the sidelines, e) is there a race on? f) Other. Explain.

Closing Prayer

Lord, your promises are true. By your grace may we all press on for the prize of the heavenly call of God in Christ Jesus. Amen.

CHAPTER 36

Passion Sunday Year C

Opening Song
Opening Prayer

Open in prayer and invite everyone to add their own prayer. Close together: "Lord, you are the king of glory, the mighty God. Hosanna in the highest. Blessed are you who comes in love and mercy. Amen."

Review Study Guidelines

First Reading   Isaiah 50:4-7a

Setting the Stage

The first reading is from the book of the prophet Isaiah. These words are first spoken about 540 years before Jesus. The Jewish people have been deported to Babylon, now known as Iraq, 50 years earlier. The person we hear speaking is called "servant of the Lord." This title can refer either to an individual, a teacher sent to bring encouragement to those people; or it can also be a symbol of the whole people suffering there in exile. *For us Christians today we can also see in these words a description of the One who suffered for us all on the cross.*

Read the first reading aloud. Reread this Scripture.
What word, phrase, or idea stands out for you?

COME TO ME

Exploring Further

1. There are four servant songs in Isaiah. How is the servant described in each?
   Isaiah 50:4
   Isaiah 42:1-2
   Isaiah 49:1-2
   Isaiah 52:13-15

2. Why does the servant know how to speak to the weary according Isaiah 50:4b?

3. How does Jesus, the Perfect Servant, know how to speak?
   Mark 6:46
   John 8:28-29
   John 12:49

4. How is the servant obedient according to Isaiah 50:5?

5. What does the servant suffer and whose help does he seek in Isaiah 50:6-7a?

6. How is Jesus treated?
   Matthew 26:67
   Matthew 27:27-31

7. Whose help does Jesus seek and how is he strengthened in Luke 22:41-43?

8. Where does Jesus go after the last supper in Luke 22:39, Sunday's gospel?

9. The fate of humanity revolves around two gardens.[53] Read Genesis 3:1-12, 23-24. Answer the following:
   Who does Adam listen to?
   What is the sin?
   What do they eat?
   Why are they hiding?
   Who seeks out man?
   What reference is made to the sword?

10. Read Luke 22:39-44, 47-51, Sunday's gospel. Answer the following questions:
    What does Jesus take upon himself?
    Whom does Jesus seek?
    How is Jesus obedient?
    How is the sword used and how does Jesus respond?

Passion Sunday Year C

What is Jesus called in 1 Corinthians 15:20?

What instrument of death is used according to 1 Peter 2:24?

Adam in the Garden of Eden:	**Jesus in the Garden of Gethsemane:**
– Adam sinned.	– Jesus took on sin.
– Adam and Eve ate the fruit forbidden	– Jesus became the first fruit.
– Adam hid from God.	– Jesus interceded with the Father
– God sought out Adam in the sin	– Jesus sought out the Father in obedience of rebellion.
– The sword is drawn to prevent entrance into the garden.	– Jesus told Peter to put away the sword he carried and healed the wound.
– Adam sinned in the garden causing death.	– Jesus ushers in redemption in the garden.
– Adam ate the fruit from the tree of knowledge of good and evil tree.	– Jesus bore our sins in his body on the tree.

11. How does Jesus refer to this time of suffering in Luke 22:53?

12. How does Jesus refer to his time of glory?
    Luke 17:24
    John 14:20
    Malachi 3:1-2
    - Satan has his hour; Jesus has his day.

13. Where is Jesus' body laid, by whom, and what is noted about this tomb in Luke 23:50-53?

A note of interest by Bishop Sheen: Jesus was born from virgin womb, laid in a virgin tomb and both betrothed by Joseph. Jesus was born in a stranger's cave and laid in a stranger's grave.

Reflection

1. Both the suffering servant in Isaiah and Jesus knew how to speak a word of comfort and wisdom because they sought the Father in prayer and listened. What does this say to you about the need to pray and to listen in prayer? Is listening part of your prayer life? Explain. What is an experience you have had of "hearing God"? When faced with a situation you did not know how to respond to, have you experienced sending a prayer for help and then words or ideas came to you? Explain.

2. Both Jesus and the servant in Isaiah suffered for the sake of others. How have you suffered for the sake of another? Was it willingly or unwillingly? What were the results?

3. When you are obedient do you expect to suffer or have things work out? Explain.

4. Jesus took on the sin of Adam; the shameful sins of Sodom and Gomorrah of the past and today. He took on the hidden sins and the sins done in the dark. He took on the sins done in the light. He took on the sins of the past and all sins of the future. Jesus took on your sin and my sin. Jesus paid a dear price to redeem us from our sin. What does he desire from us in return?

5. (Put your name in the following blanks.) (Your name) sinned and hid from God. God sought out (your name). (Your name) lost unity with God. Jesus took on (your name)'s sin. Jesus interceded and brought redemption to (your name).

6. In what ways do we hide from God? How has God sought you out?

Optional Exercise before the second reading. Have each person in the group briefly tell something of their past week or of an event anticipated in the coming week. This could be a time to share a triumph, a trial, or a need.

Second Reading   Philippians 2:5-11

Setting the Stage

This reading is from the letter of St. Paul to the church at Philippi, northern Greece. He is writing from a prison, perhaps in western Turkey, about 30 years after the resurrection of Jesus. The Philippians sent help to Paul and he writes to thank them and to encourage them in their faith. This reading is actually a quote from an early Christian hymn.[54] Note these two phrases: 1. "The same mind," which means "the same attitude"; and 2. "Under the earth." which refers to a place of the dead, that is, to all those who have died.[55] The question is: *through these words, whose attitude is God our Father calling us to imitate?*

Read this reading aloud. Reread this Scripture.
What word, phrase, or idea stands out for you?

Exploring Further

1. What is the mind of Christ according to Philippians 2:5-7?

2. Who is Jesus according to the following?
John 1:1-4
John 10:2-5, 7-10

Passion Sunday Year C

    Colossians 1:15-20
    Hebrews 1:3-4

3. What is Jesus' attitude according to the following Scriptures?
   Philippians 2:8
   2 Corinthians 8:9
   Matthew 20:28

4. What is the result of his obedience?
   Philippians 2:9-11
   Ephesians 1:20-23
   Revelation 5:1-5, 12-14

5. What is our hope if we believe and are obedient?
   Matthew 25:34-36
   Ephesians 1:13-14
   Hebrews 9:15
   1 Peter 1:3-7

Reflection

1. Jesus does not cling to his position or power or glory but he becomes poor for our sake and he comes to serve, lead us, and give us life. What position(s) do you have and what people do you have some power over? What advantages and responsibilities go along with this position? What advantages, rights, or privileges of your position could you let go of and how might you serve and give to others?

2. Jesus gives everything and then is lifted up and exalted. What reward awaits those who obediently follow Jesus and surrender everything? Does the promise of this reward help you remain faithful? Why or why not?

Closing Prayer

Lord, you humble yourself for our sake. May we follow your example and share in your resurrection. Amen.

SECTION FIVE

EASTER

Easter is the culmination of all our faith, hopes, beliefs, and dreams.

We celebrate Easter for 50 days. The number '49' [7x7] stands for the fullness of time for the Jewish people. The church adds one more day, making 50, to show Easter is greater than the fullness of time. We need the 40 days of Lent to empty ourselves and prepare in order to recognize and celebrate the 50 days of Easter.

A number of years ago my good friend Gail made the comment that we will fast and do penance for forty days, but we are not up to celebrating for fifty days. In part, it is hard to sustain the celebration because we do not really grasp what it means to be an Easter people, a "resurrection people." We are more comfortable with the cross and the pain of life than the hope and freedom of the resurrection. Gail decided that every Easter season she would pick pussy willows and have fresh flowers displayed throughout Easter as a reminder to keep celebrating. Only a few years later Gail died of cancer. I now have pussy willows and fresh flowers throughout the Easter season to celebrate Gail's resurrection and to remember that I am part of a "resurrection people," and that this is our time to celebrate.

Easter teaches us that even in the face of pain, suffering, and death we believe in things not yet seen. We have a sure hope in the promises of life, hope, salvation, and joy.

I want to challenge you to be an Easter people, an alleluia people, to live as a people full of hope and joy because Jesus has risen! Indeed, he has risen. So will we. Celebrate the six Sundays of Easter, Ascension Sunday, and Pentecost. Celebrate for 50 days!

After Easter we are led back into ordinary time by two more feast days. First, we have Trinity Sunday when we are reminded that our one God subsists in Three Persons, the Father, Son, and Holy Spirit. The Trinity gives us the perfect example of living in a loving community which always produces life. The second feast day is that of the Body and Blood of Christ, or Corpus Christi Sunday. At this feast we remember how we are nourished and sustained for the spiritual journey.

We come full circle back to ordinary time; the daily routine that is so necessary to the faith journey. Here we develop life lessons of prayer, study, and service, gathering as a people. In routine, we develop a foundational relationship with God, strengthening us to stand firm during the celebrating times and the sorrowing times of life.

*Repent and be baptized every one
Of you in the name of Jesus Christ . . .
and you will receive
the gift of the Holy Spirit.*

(Acts 2:38)

CHAPTER 37

Easter Sunday Year C

Opening Song
Opening Prayer

Open in prayer and invite everyone to add their own prayer. Close together: "Lord, let our hearts burn as we hear your word and open our eyes to your presence among us. Amen."

Review Study Guidelines

Gospel   Luke 24:13-35

For the Easter Bible study we will study the gospel. This is an account of Jesus appearing to the disciples on the road to Emmaus.

Read the gospel aloud. Reread this Scripture.
What word, phrase, or idea stands out for you?

Exploring Further

1. As the disciples travel to Emmaus, what events are being discussed?
   Luke 24:1-14
   Luke 24:19-20

2. What happens in Luke 24:15-16?

Come to Me

3. With what word or sign is Jesus recognized?
   Luke 24:36-43
   John 20:13-16
   John 20:19-20
   John 21:4-7
   John 21:9-13

4. How is Jesus described in Luke 24:19?

5. Who do the people say Jesus is?
   Matthew 16:14
   Luke 7:16
   John 9:17

6. What are the Hebrew people waiting for according to Matthew 17:1-3, 5, 9-12?

7. How is this prophesy fulfilled according to Matthew 11:7-15

8. Following the return of the spirit of Elijah, what is to come?
   Luke 24:21a
   Luke 1:67-75
   Luke 2:25, 27-32, 36, 38

9. What news is the hardest for the disciples to believe in Luke 24:21b-24?

10. What does Jesus say about believing the prophets?
    Luke 24:25
    Luke 16:29-31

11. What has been foretold and how are the disciples prepared for the passion of Jesus?
    Luke 24:26
    Luke 9:22
    Luke 18:31-33
    1 Peter 1:10-11

12. What does Jesus teach these two disciples in Luke 24:27?

13. What are some of the Old Testament promises Jesus fulfills?
    Acts 2:29-31
    Acts 3:22

Easter Sunday Year C

Acts 4:11-12

Acts 13:32-34

14. When do the disciples recognize Jesus in Luke 24:30-31?

15. What effect did the sharing of Scriptures have on the disciples in Luke 24:32?

16. What is the result of the disciples' encounter with the risen Jesus in Luke 24:33-35?

Reflection

1. The disciples were in a lively exchange over the events of Jesus' death and reported resurrection. What topic has caused lively debate in your circles lately? What lively exchange regarding Jesus, his life, his power, etc., have you been involved in?

2. The disciples recognized Jesus: in the breaking of the bread; by allowing them to touch him; by showing them his wounds; calling them by name; and by repeating past events of throwing out the nets for fish and cooking breakfast for them. In what events have you recognized Jesus and experienced the reality of the risen Jesus?

3. Though the coming of Jesus, his suffering, death and resurrection were foretold and awaited, the Israelites did not recognize or understand Jesus and his life. How can we fail to understand promises of God and gifts of God to us, especially if they come in a package of suffering? How can we grow in faith and trust of God with every detail of our lives?

4. Jesus taught the disciples and opened their minds to understand the Scriptures. How can we grow in our understanding of Scriptures? Why do you think it is important to have this understanding of Scripture?

5. After the disciples experienced the grace of awakening they were excited and left immediately to tell the others the good news. How have your moments of awakening to the risen Jesus prompted you to share with others?

6. John Paul II said, "The beginning of the Christian journey is an encounter with the risen Lord." After a spiritual awakening the journey begins; the adventure starts. What adventures has your Christian journey brought your way?

Optional Exercise before the second reading. Have each person in the group briefly tell something of their past week or of an event anticipated in the coming week. This could be a time to share a triumph, a trial, or a need.

Closing Prayer

Alleluia, the Lord has risen; he is risen indeed! Risen Jesus, we desire an encounter with you. Draw us in to the exciting adventure of serving you with our lives, of sharing the good news with others. Bring your people to the glory of the resurrection. Amen.

CHAPTER 38

SECOND SUNDAY OF EASTER
DIVINE MERCY SUNDAY
YEAR C

OPENING SONG
OPENING PRAYER

Open in prayer and invite everyone to add their own prayer. Close together: "Rejoice to the full in the glory that is yours, and give thanks to God who is merciful and called you to his kingdom. Alleluia."

REVIEW STUDY GUIDELINES

First Reading   Acts 5:12-16

Setting the Stage

During the Easter Season, that is, from Easter Sunday until Pentecost, the 50th day, we hear as first reading portions of the Acts of the Apostles. This is written by St. Luke as a sequel to the gospel of Jesus that he had published earlier. We hear of what happens to the apostles after that first Easter and Pentecost. In this reading we see them in the place called the Portico of Solomon, which is part of the Jewish temple in Jerusalem. Thus they still consider themselves as members of the Jewish community. *The questions addressed here are: Is coming together and sticking together an important part of being a follower of Jesus? Do I see the awesomeness of it?*

Read the first reading aloud. Reread this Scripture.
What word, phrase, or idea stands out for you?

Come to Me

Exploring Further

1. In this summary, what is stressed in Acts 5:12?

2. As people witnessed the faithful gathering and the miracles, what was the result in Acts 5:14?

3. How are the sick healed according to Acts 5:15?

4. How is this similar to what is recorded in the following Scriptures?
   Acts 19:12
   Mark 6:56

5. How does Jesus prepare the disciples for this time in John 20:19-23, 30-31, Sunday's gospel?

6. As word spreads, what is the result in Acts 5:16?

7. If you have never witnessed this type of dramatic miracle, how do Jesus' words comfort you in John 20:24-29, Sunday's gospel?

Reflection

1. In your faith journey, what people or activities first attracted you? Explain.

2. In your faith journey now, what supports, encourages, and inspires you to continue?

3. What physical or spiritual healing have you experienced?

Optional Exercise before the second reading. Have each person in the group briefly tell something of their past week or of an event anticipated in the coming week. This could be a time to share a triumph, a trial, or a need.

Second Sunday of Easter Divine Mercy Sunday Year C

Second Reading   Revelation 1:9-13, 17-19

Setting the Stage

From now until the feast of the Ascension as a second reading at Sunday masses we shall be hearing portions of the book of Revelation. This is written about 70 years after the resurrection of Jesus by a certain person named John during a terrible persecution by the Roman Empire. The author in fact is exiled to a tiny island off the west coast of Turkey, called Patmos, which is used by the Romans as a penal colony. He describes here a vision he has of Jesus. These words are written to Christians in seven churches, symbolized by seven lamp stands. A question being addressed is: *In my difficult moments, who do I turn to?*

Read this reading aloud. Reread this Scripture.
What word, phrase, or idea stands out for you?

Exploring Further

1. Where is the author writing from and why is he there according to Revelation 1:9?

2. What do we learn about endurance and discipleship from the following verses?
   Romans 5:3-5
   2 Timothy 2:12?

3. What day of the week is it and what happens to John according to Revelation 1:10?

4. Who is this letter written for according to Revelation 1:11?

5. How is Jesus described in Revelation 1:12-16?
   Note what the following symbolize:
   – the long robe symbolizes his priesthood
   – the golden cord round the waist his royalty
   – the white hair his eternity
   – the burning eyes (to probe minds and 'hearts') symbolize his divine knowledge
   – the feet of bronze his permanence
   – the brightness of his legs and face, and the strength of voice symbolizes the fear inspired by his majesty[56]
   – the double edged sword is a symbol of judgement on faithless Christians

6. How does this description compare to Daniel's vision?
   Daniel 7:9-10
   Daniel 10:5-6

7. At this sight of the Son of Man, what does John do in Revelation 1:17a?

8. How is this response partially explained in Exodus 33:20?

9. How is John reassured in Revelation 1:17b?

10. What core truth of our Christian faith does Jesus affirm in Revelation 1:18?

11. Because Jesus lives, what hope does this give us according to Hebrews 7:24-25?

Reflection

1. If today Christians were being exiled to Patmos for proclaiming the word and witnessing to Jesus, would you be exiled? Why or why not?

2. After understanding what the symbols used to describe Jesus mean, what picture of Jesus do you have from this reading? Does it change how you previously thought of Jesus? Explain.

3. The book of Revelation is written during terrible persecution. These early Christians are encouraged to be faithful, even if the cost is martyrdom, while waiting patiently and with hope for the victorious return of Christ as King and Lord. In our day, what might be a result of Christians being faithless and not standing firm? What are examples and results of Christians being faithful and standing firm in faith and hope?

4. Jesus says to each of us today, "fear not, I live." To what situation in your life does this give comfort or hope? Explain.

Closing Prayer

Lord, help us to be faithful in proclaiming your word and to be a joyful witness to the risen Savior. Thank you for your startling gift of divine mercy that you pour out upon the world. Help us approach this great sea of mercy. Amen.

CHAPTER 39

THIRD SUNDAY OF EASTER YEAR C

OPENING SONG
OPENING PRAYER

Open in prayer and invite everyone to add their own prayer. Close together: "Lord, help us always to put obedience to God before obedience to human authority and give us the grace to rejoice when we suffer for the sake of your name. Amen."

REVIEW STUDY GUIDELINES

First Reading   Acts 5:27-32, 40b-41

Setting the Stage

The first reading is from the Acts of the Apostles. Last Sunday we saw the reaction of the ordinary people when the apostles first started talking about the resurrection of Jesus. Today we see the reaction of the high priest and the council, which is similar to our Supreme Court for the Jewish people. A question for us to consider is: *when I am under pressure to deny my faith, what do I do?*

Read the first reading aloud. Reread this Scripture.
What word, phrase, or idea stands out for you?

Exploring Further

1. What happened to the apostles the previous night according to Acts 5:17-18?

Come to Me

2. When the temple police go to bring the apostles before the council, where do they find the apostles and how do they come to be there according to Acts 5:19-26?

3. What is the council's concern in Acts 5:27-28?

4. What does the name of Jesus mean according to Matthew 1:21, 23?

5. When ordered to stop preaching in the name of Jesus, how do the apostles reply?
   Acts 5:29
   Acts 4:19-2

6. The earliest apostolic discourses contain the following basic elements.[57] Which of these elements can you identify in the apostolic discourse in Acts 5:30-32?
   a. A witness to the death and resurrection and exultation of Jesus.
   b. Certain details of Jesus' ministry inaugurated by teaching and miracle and completed by appearances of the risen Christ and by the gift of the Spirit.
   c. It places the story in the wider setting, connecting to the Old Testament and the fulfillment of the prophecies, the advent of the messianic era, invitation to repentance for the forgiveness of sins before the Christ's glorious return.

7. How does the council decide to proceed with dealing with the apostles and why in Acts 5:34-39?

8. What happens to the apostles as a result of this decision in Acts 5:40?

9. How do the apostles respond to this and why, according to Acts 5:41-42?

10. What are believers willing to do and why?
    Acts 21:13
    1 Peter 4:14-19
    3 John 5-8

11. How does Jesus prepare his disciples for what is to come?
    Matthew 5:10-12
    Matthew 10:17
    John 15:20-21

12. What experience do the apostles have and how might this experience help them to face hard times "for the sake of his name" in John 21:1-14, Sunday's gospel?

Third Sunday of Easter Year C

13. What experiences does Peter have and what do you think he learns from these experiences that helps him in his ministry "for the sake of his name"?
    John 18:25-27
    John 21:15-19 (Sunday's gospel)

Reflection

1. Have you ever been ordered to stop proclaiming or witnessing in the name of Jesus? Explain. How do you witness and proclaim in the name of Jesus? If someone protested would you quickly stop? Why or why not?

2. Where do people today suffer abuse, persecution, flogging, imprisonment, or insult for the sake of His name? What would you be willing to do for the "sake of his name"?

3. The first time Peter received pressure for being a follower of Jesus, he denied Jesus. After the resurrection, Jesus extended love, mercy, and forgiveness to Peter and sent him out to lead and feed his people. Peter received the Holy Spirit and remained faithful, giving his life for "the sake of his name." What experience of God have you had that you can remember and draw strength from in the event of suffering or persecution or abuse for being a follower of Jesus Christ?

Optional Exercise before the second reading. Have each person in the group briefly tell something of their past week or of an event anticipated in the coming week. This could be a time to share a triumph, a trial, or a need.

Second Reading   Revelation 5:11-14

Setting the Stage

The second reading is from the book of Revelation. This is written about 70 years after the resurrection of Jesus, during a time of persecution by the Roman Empire. A man named John is the author, and in this reading he describes a vision he has of heaven. The book is written to encourage those early Christians; but it has many symbols, a kind of code language. This is to prevent it being confiscated by the authorities. The symbols we hear of today are:

1. *The Lamb* is a symbol of Jesus who sacrificed his life for us.
2. *Four living creatures* are symbols of all created things.[58]
3. *Elders* are a symbols of priests offering praise and adoration.

Come to Me

Through these words, God our Father is telling us *the place Jesus has in the life of his people on earth and in heaven.*

Read the second reading aloud. Reread this Scripture.
What word, phrase, or idea stands out for you?

Exploring Further

1. What is happening in Revelation 5:11-12?

2. Who is singing in Revelation 5:11?

3. What does the early church sing in Philippians 2:9-11?

4. What are they singing in Revelation 5:13?

5. How do the living creatures and elders respond in Revelation 5:14?

6. What is our hope and the promise given us?
   Ephesians 2:4-7
   Colossians 2:12-14
   Colossians 3:2-4

Reflection

1. God humbled himself and came to us as a man. He was persecuted, insulted, flogged, and crucified to free us from sin and give us everlasting life. Following his suffering and death, Jesus was resurrected, exalted, and forever is worshipped. In the first reading, we read how we too can expect suffering, persecution, insult, flogging, imprisonment, and death as a result of following Jesus. If we are faithful, what can we hope for? Is the promise and hope of heaven enough to keep you faithful in difficult circumstances, trials, and temptations? Explain.

2. The gift of salvation is free to all who would receive it and cannot be bought or earned. Once we receive this gift, it costs us everything! We now belong to Jesus, body and soul. How do you understand this seeming paradox? How can we explain to others why it is worth surrendering all to be a follower of Jesus? What is the alternative?

3. Often people get excited when they first come to faith but when hard times come or as time elapses, they grow cold and fall away. Do we always make the cost clear? Why do you think so? Can you think of times on your Christian journey that you considered it hard work? Explain. How and why did you keep going? What have been the rewards?

4. Since we will spend eternity worshipping and praising God, we should practice on earth. Any acknowledgment of God and service for God can be an act of worship. In this past week, what are you thankful for, grateful for, have received or given that you want to now offer back to God?

Closing Prayer

Worthy is the Lamb that was slaughtered to receive power and wealth, wisdom and strength, honor and glory and blessing! Amen.

CHAPTER 40

Fourth Sunday of Easter Year C

Opening Song
Opening Prayer

Open in prayer and invite everyone to add their own prayer. Close together: "Lord, we are your people, the sheep of your flock. Thank you for your faithful, enduring love. Amen."

Review Study Guidelines

First Reading   Acts 13:14, 43-52

Setting the Stage

The first reading is from the Acts of the Apostles, which is written by St. Luke. We hear about St. Paul and St. Barnabas on their first missionary journey, which takes place from 46 to 49 AD. They sail from the city of Antioch in Syria to Cyprus, and then go into what is now Central Turkey, to a town with the same name as the city they start from, called Antioch, in the province of Pisidia. We see the standard procedure of St. Paul on first entering a town: first he goes to the Jewish synagogue showing how Jesus fulfilled the Jewish prophecies. The reactions are always very similar, so then we see what he does. Note the word "Gentiles." This is a technical word that means persons who are not Jews. A question being addressed here is: *When we try to live as God our Father wants us to, do we expect to be welcomed without criticism?*

Read the first reading aloud. Reread this Scripture.
What word, phrase, or idea stands out for you?

Come to Me

Exploring Further

1. Upon arriving in Pisidia, where does Paul go first in Acts 13:14?

2. What is Paul invited to do in Acts 13:15?

3. What is the result of Paul's speaking in Acts 13:42-43?

4. Who shows up the following Sabbath according to Acts 13:44?

5. What grips the leaders and how do they react as a result in Acts 13:45?

6. How do Paul and Barnabas respond and what door does this open in Acts 13:46?

7. What prophesy from Isaiah is being fulfilled in Acts 13:47?

8. Who is the light according to John 8:12?

9. What is the light according to Psalm 119:105?

10. Who is the light according to Matthew 5:14-16?

11. How do the Gentiles respond in Acts 13:48-49?

12. What does Jesus say about hearing him in John 10:27-30, Sunday's gospel?

13. How do the Jews react in Acts 13:50?

14. What symbolic action do Paul and Barnabas perform in Acts 13:51?

15. What does this signify according to Luke 9:5?

16. What characterizes the disciples in their work in Acts 13:52?

Reflection

1. When the crowds responded to Paul's message, the Jewish leaders were jealous. Can you think of a time you experienced jealousy and how it made you act? Explain. Within the body of Christ, what are potential causes for jealousy? How can we guard against jealousy and instead rejoice in God's work, no matter who is doing it or how it comes about?

Fourth Sunday of Easter Year C

2. Can you think of a time that Jesus, his word, or his people have brought light into your life? Explain.

3. Have you faced opposition because of your faith from community leaders or family? Explain.

4. The people in Antioch listened to Paul and Barnabas and then listened to the officials. Jesus said his sheep listen to His voice. There are many voices today competing to be heard. Where do we hear Jesus' voice? What voices compete with this message of truth and how do they distract and mislead?

Optional Exercise before the second reading. Have each person in the group briefly tell something of their past week or of an event anticipated in the coming week. This could be a time to share a triumph, a trial, or a need.

Second Reading   Revelation 7:9, 14-17

Setting the Stage

The second reading is from the book of Revelation. This book is written about the year 100 AD when the Roman Empire is persecuting Christians who refuse to worship Roman gods. Through these words, written by John, God our Father wants to encourage His people. This book has many symbols:
1. The lamb is Jesus
2. Palms are a symbol for victory
3. "Washing robes in the blood of the Lamb" is a symbol of the effectiveness of the death of Jesus.[59]

A question for us to think about as we listen is: *What is at the end of the road of life for those who "hang in" with the Lord?*

Read the second reading aloud. Reread this Scripture.
What word, phrase, or idea stands out for you?

Exploring Further

1. Who is assembled in this heavenly scene according to Revelation 7:9?

2. What promise does this fulfill from Genesis 15:5?

COME TO ME

3. In what conditions do these people remain faithful according to Revelation 7:14a?

4. For the faithful, what does the blood of Jesus do in Revelation 7:14b?

5. How is this prophesied in Daniel 12:1?

6. How will joy and gratitude be expressed in heaven according to Revelation 7:15a?

7. What is the promise to the Israelites according to the following verses?
   Isaiah 25:8
   Isaiah 49:8-11?
   Eschatology: doctrine of last things, dealing with such things as death, resurrection, second coming of Christ, end of the age, divine judgment, and the future state.[60] The cessation of *hunger, thirst* and intense *heat* allude to the idyllic eschatological conditions described in Isaiah.49:10[61]

8. How will the people be cared for in Revelation 7:15b-16?

9. What is the Shepherd described doing in Revelation 7:17?

10. How does Jesus refer to himself in John 4:13-14 and John 6:35?

11. What does the Shepherd Jesus tell us in John 10:27-30, Sunday's gospel?

12. How is the absence of sorrow described and who wipes away the tears in Revelation 7:17?

Reflection

1. Does this glimpse of heaven help you and give you hope for the hard events you experience here on earth? Why or why not?

2. Where today are people persecuted, oppressed, and killed for their faith? What are possible ways we can help the persecuted church?

Closing Prayer

Lord, for the persecuted church today, we ask you to pour out your grace, refreshment, and hope. Help us to know how we can help. In all our struggles, keep the hope of what you have prepared alive in our hearts. Amen.

CHAPTER 41

Fifth Sunday of Easter Year C

Opening Song
Opening Prayer

Open in prayer and invite everyone to add their own prayer. Close together: "Lord, by your grace, teach us to love one another as you have loved us. Amen."

Review Study Guidelines

First Reading   Acts 14:21-27

Setting the Stage

The first reading is from the Acts of the Apostles. We hear of St. Paul and Barnabas completing their first mission in what is now central Turkey. They retrace their steps, revisiting the churches they have just set up. The year is 49 AD. We hear the ancient names of many places, two of which are cities with the same name: Antioch, the first one in Turkey and the second in Syria. Through these words, God our Father is telling us the *cost of belonging to His family*.

Read the first reading aloud. Reread this Scripture.
What word, phrase, or idea stands out for you?

Exploring Further

1. Why do Paul and Barnabas return to the churches they established according to Acts 14:22?

2. What do the following Scriptures show about the diligence of Paul's work?
   Acts 11:25-26
   Acts 15:30-32
   Acts 18:23

3. What happened to Paul on his previous visit to Lystra according to Acts 14:19-20?

4. In the following Scriptures, what is clearly a part of proclaiming the kingdom?
   Acts 14:22b
   Matthew 10:16-18, 22
   2 Timothy 3:10-12
   Hebrews 10:32-36

5. What is the value and reward of suffering?
   Romans 5:3-5
   2 Thessalonians 1:4-7
   2 Timothy 2:10-13

6. What church structure do they establish in Acts 14:23?

7. As Paul too is under church order, what does he report back to the church in Antioch who sent him on this missionary journey, according to Acts 14:27?

8. How might Paul and Barnabas have been strengthened and encouraged according to the information given in Acts 14:27-28?

9. What command does Jesus give in John 13:34-35, Sunday's gospel?

10. How do Paul and Barnabas demonstrate this commandment in the Scriptures read today?

Reflection

1. In the past week, have you been an encourager or a complainer? How do you respond when you hear others complain? Recently, who has encouraged and strengthened you?

2. Paul and Barnabas experienced persecution and rejection and now want the new Christians to be prepared for this same experience. What are practical ways we can prepare to face rejection and persecution in an appropriate manner?

3. Paul and Barnabas are diligent and faithful in caring for the churches they establish. Despite hardship they build up, encourage, strengthen, teach, and train others to carry on leadership. In your

vocation, where do you need to be diligent, careful, and faithful? Who are you responsible to encourage, strengthen, and teach? Are there others to whom you need to delegate leadership? Why or why not?

4. Whose order or authority or leadership are you under? Do you see this as a blessing and safeguard, or as a restriction? Why?

Optional Exercise before the second reading. Have each person in the group briefly tell something of their past week or of an event anticipated in the coming week. This could be a time to share a triumph, a trial, or a need.

Second Reading   Revelation 21:1-5a

Setting the Stage

The second reading is from the book of Revelation written by John about the year 100 AD. This is a time of persecution by the Roman Empire so the book is written as an encouragement to Christians. Many symbols are used. This is to avoid its being outlawed by civil authorities. The symbols in today's reading are:
1. The sea. Because of its terrible storms, it became a symbol of violence and evil.
2. The holy city, the New Jerusalem. This is a symbol of us, the people of God.
3. Heaven here is used to mean the sky and the galaxies.

The question being addressed is: *Will unfairness one day be replaced with fairness?*

Read the second reading aloud. Reread this Scripture.
What word, phrase, or idea stands out for you?

Exploring Further

1. How is God's eternal kingdom described?
   Revelation 21:1
   Isaiah 65:17
   2 Peter 3:13

2. How does Paul describe the waiting for the new heaven and earth in Romans 8:19-23?

3. What analogy for the coming of the kingdom is used?
   Revelation 21:2
   Revelation 19:7-8

4. How is the coming of the kingdom foretold in Isaiah?
   Isaiah 7:14
   Isaiah 9:5-6
   Isaiah 11:1-9

5. Who is at the center of the kingdom according to Revelation 21:3?

6. How will things be in the heavenly kingdom according to Revelation 21:4-5a?

7. How does this new kingdom come to be?
   John 1:31-35 (Sunday's gospel)
   2 Corinthians 5:17-18

Reflection

1. Consider the following:

   The apostle [Paul] speaks of the whole Church and of each of the faithful, as a bride "betrothed" to Christ the Lord so as to become but one spirit with him. The Church is the spotless bride of the spotless Lamb. Christ loved the Church and gave himself up for her, that he might sanctify her. He has joined himself to her in an everlasting covenant and never stops caring for her as for his own body.[62]

   Our heavenly vocation will be to be the bride of Christ for all eternity. What does this mean to you? How can we prepare now for this vocation?

2. What comes to mind when you think of heaven as your hometown or permanent home that Jesus has prepared for you?

3. God pours love in our hearts through the Holy Spirit. We receive this love and pour out love on God and others by word, deed, suffering, and laying down our lives. How does living this way bring about the kingdom of God now? What will be added or more complete when Jesus returns?

Closing Prayer

Merciful Father, may these mysteries give us new purpose and bring us to a new life in you. Amen.

CHAPTER 42

Sixth Sunday of Easter
Year C

Opening Song
Opening Prayer

Open in prayer and invite everyone to add their own prayer. Close together: "Father, thank you for sending your Holy Spirit to guide your people in the way of truth. Amen."

Review Study Guidelines

First Reading — Acts 15:1-2, 22-29

Setting the Stage

The first reading is from the Acts of the Apostles. We hear of the biggest question the first Christians faced. It is this—if you are not a Jew, that is, if you are a Gentile, and you want to become a follower of Jesus, do you need to be circumcised and follow all the Jewish customs? To solve the problem, the first big meeting of the church, the Council of Jerusalem, is convened. The year is 49 AD. Today's reading has two parts. The first part is the calling of the Council. The second part is the decree, the letter that is formulated after the discussion. To respect the sensitivities of the Christians of Jewish background who live and eat together with their fellow Christians who are not of Jewish background, the apostles came up with guidelines. These include: 1. No marriage to close relatives. Such a relationship is called "fornication" in this Bible text. 2. No eating of blood or strangled animals, because the blood would still be in them. Blood is a symbol of life and no one except God our Father has power over life, especially human life.

COME TO ME

Read the first reading aloud. Reread this Scripture.
What word, phrase, or idea stands out for you?

Exploring Further

1. What are some people teaching the Antioch church in Acts 15:1?

2. How do Paul and Barnabus react and what solution is reached in Acts 15:2?

3. How is this delegation received by the Jerusalem church in Acts 15:4?

4. What is the response to their question on circumcision in Acts 15:5-6?

5. What is Peter's position in Acts 15:7-11?

6. How is this revealed to Peter in Acts 10:44-48?

7. What do Paul and Barnabus confirm in Acts 15:12?

8. What does James declare and what is the verdict in Acts 15:13-17?

9. How is this verdict to be made known to the church in Antioch according to Acts 15:22?

10. Why does the dispute arise in the first place according the Acts 15:24?

11. What is the role of Judas and Silas according to Acts 15:27?

12. Who made this decision according to Acts 15:28?

13. Why are the disciples confident in saying "the Holy Spirit and we decided"?
    John 14:23-28 (Sunday's gospel)
    John 16:12-15

Reflection

The Council of Jerusalem was the first council of the church. The following is a list of the main church councils over the years.

- The Council of Nicea in 325 dealt with the heresy that denied the divinity of Christ.
- The Council of Ephesus in 431 established that Mary is the Mother of God.
- The Council of Chalcedon in 451 stressed that Christ's divine and human natures are united in one person.

Sixth Sunday of Easter Year C

- The Council of Trent in 1545 to 1563 was convened by Paul III after the reformation and defined Catholic teaching regarding faith and interpretation of Scriptures, and corrected abuses and improved the training of priests.
- The First Vatican Council in 1870 declared the doctrine of Papal Infallibility.
- The Second Vatican Council from 1962 to 1965 convened by John XXIII encouraged lay participation in the Mass and the use of the vernacular, reconciliation with the Eastern Church and extended friendship to protestant denominations and Jews.

The church faces challenges in every age and gathers the bishops and leaders together to discuss pray and seek the Holy Spirit. The above councils are a gathering of the whole church. Regionally the bishops also meet to discuss challenges they face. Today the Church in China, Rwanda, and Cuba face persecution. Haiti and the Balkans face crumbling societies and the western countries face the cheapening of life that comes from an emphasis on material gain.[63]

1. The Canadian and American bishops have made many statements on issues of concern in our countries. What issues have these bishops spoken about that you are aware of? Do you see these statements as the Holy Spirit guiding the church in a similar way to the decision made following the Council of Jerusalem in today's reading? Why or why not?

2. Do you accept the decisions of the church leaders through councils, synods, encyclicals, or statements following a conference as truth for the church? Why or why not?

3. As the Gentiles became believers, discernment was needed as to what was a matter of faith and morals and what was cultural tradition. What might be examples of cultural practices in our faith that may be different in other countries? What are examples in our faith of essentials that do not change with culture?

4. Dissension arose from certain people presenting their own agenda. How can we be clear on what is church teaching and what is the agenda of a select group within the church?

Optional Exercise before the second reading. Have each person in the group briefly tell something of their past week or of an event anticipated in the coming week. This could be a time to share a triumph, a trial, or a need.

Second Reading   Revelation 21:10-14, 22-23

Setting the Stage

The second reading is from the book of Revelation. The author writes about the year 100 AD when the Roman Empire is persecuting the early Christians. He describes a vision of better things to come. He uses a kind of code language which prevents the book from being confiscated by the authorities. The codes or symbols used here are:

1. The Lamb—signifying Jesus.
2. Jerusalem—a symbol of all of us who are the people of God, past, present, and future.
3. The number "12"—a symbol of completeness, of continuity of all God's people before and after Jesus.

A question being addressed is: *in our moments of pain, what do we hope for?*

Read the second reading aloud. Reread this Scripture.
What word, phrase, or idea stands out for you?

Exploring Further

1. What will the angel show John in Revelation 21:9?

2. Who is the bride of the Lamb according to Revelation 21:10?

3. How is the beauty of the bride, the New Jerusalem, the church, described in Revelation 21:11-12?

4. How is the New Jerusalem described in Isaiah 60:1-3?

5. What is the foundation of the New Jerusalem according to Revelation 21:14?

6. The number 12 shows perfection and completeness. What are there 12 of in Revelation 21:12-14?

7. What is the center of earthly worship that is no more in the New Jerusalem according to Revelation 21:22a?

Sixth Sunday of Easter Year C

8. What replaces the earthly temple?
   Revelation 21:22b
   John 2:19-21
   Ephesians 2:19-22

9. What gives light to the city in Revelation 21:23?

10. What is taking place in believers according to 2 Corinthians 3:18?

Reflection

1. Many times over the years the glory of God has been dimly reflected in the church through sin, abuse of power and authority, and apathy of God's people. What hope does the description of the bride of the Lamb, the church, in Revelation give you? How does our cooperation with God or lack of it make a difference to the glory of God in his church?

2. There is no longer a temple to go to in the New Jerusalem. Jesus is the temple. The church is not a place to go to but is us, all the people of God. What image does this glimpse of eternity give you?

Closing Prayer

Lord, we are the bride of the Lamb. We turn our eyes to you to be transformed more and more into your image. Amen.

CHAPTER 43

Ascension Sunday Year C

Opening Song
Opening Prayer

Open in prayer and invite everyone to add their own prayer. Close together: "Lord, you ascended to the Father where you intercede on our behalf. Help us be faithful to the mission you left us until your return. Amen."

Review Study Guidelines

First Reading   Acts 1:1-11

Setting the Stage

This year, the gospel reading on most of the Sundays is from the gospel of Jesus according to St. Luke. During the Easter season, the first reading is from the Acts of the Apostles, also written by St. Luke, as a sequel to his first book. And something interesting happens today: We have the very end of his gospel book and the very beginning of the second book. We can see how closely they are linked. In this reading we are given two biblical symbols from the Old Testament— "clouds" and being "lifted up." They describe the presence of God and his world of heaven. There is also an allusion to the prophet Elisha, who lived about 850 years before Jesus. Elisha was able to catch a glimpse of his teacher, Elijah, being lifted up to heaven and so is able to have a share of his teaching spirit. It is easy to see the reason why the beginning of the Acts of the Apostles is read on this feast of the Ascension of the Lord Jesus.

Note the name "Theophilus." It is a Greek name meaning "a lover of God." It is possibly the name of the Christian who helps St. Luke distribute the books, or, could we say that each one of us is a "theophilus?"

Come to Me

Read the first reading aloud. Reread this Scripture.
What word, phrase, or idea stands out for you?

Exploring Further

1. What is Luke's purpose in writing?
   Acts 1:1-2
   Luke 1:1-4

2. What happens after Jesus' suffering and for how long according to Acts 1:3?

3. How did the following examples convince and remove doubt of the resurrection?
   Matthew 28:8-10
   Luke 24:36-43

4. What are Jesus' instructions and why are they to wait?
   Acts 1:4-5
   John 15:26-27
   John 16:7-15

5. What does the disciples' response indicate in Acts 1:6?

6. What is Jesus' response and what is he referring to?
   Acts 1:7
   Mark 13:26-27, 32-33
   1 Thessalonians 5:1-2

7. What are Jesus' final instructions?
   Acts 1:8
   Luke 24:46-49 (Sunday's gospel)
   Matthew 28:18-20

8. What takes place after these instructions?
   Acts 1:9
   Luke 24:50-51 (Sunday's gospel)

9. What similarities to the ascension take place in 2 Kings 2:11-15?

10. Who appears to the disciples and what do they tell them in Acts 1:10-11?

11. What do the following verses teach us about the return of Jesus?
    Matthew 26:64

Ascension Sunday Year C

   Mark 13:26-27
   1 Thessalonians 4:16-17

12. What do the disciples do after the ascension?
    Acts 1:12-14
    Luke 24:52-53 (Sunday's gospel)

Reflection

1. St. Luke set about to write an orderly account of the life, ministry, and death of Jesus and then of the life and works of the early church. If you were to set about to write an orderly account of your spiritual journey, what are several points you would include? What are several points that an orderly account of your church community would include in covering the past ten to thirty years?

2. Imagine the roller-coaster of emotions the disciples went through in a short time with Judas' betrayal, Jesus suffering and death, the excitement and shock at seeing him alive again, being commissioned to witness to the whole world, then his leaving with the promise to send the comforter, the Holy Spirit for strength and guidance. Think of a time in your life when you experienced a roller-coaster of emotions. How was your suffering or being overwhelmed relieved and what gave you hope and comfort?

3. The promise not to be left alone and that Jesus will return is for us today just as it was for the disciples. What does this promise mean to you? Why do you think Jesus had to ascend to the Father in order to be with us always?

Optional Exercise before the second reading. Have each person in the group briefly tell something of their past week or of an event anticipated in the coming week. This could be a time to share a triumph, a trial, or a need.

Come to Me

Second Reading   Hebrews 9:24-28, 10:19-23

Setting the Stage

The second reading is from the letter to the Hebrews written about 40 years after the resurrection of Jesus. The author is a Christian of Jewish background who is inspired by God our Father to write to other Jewish Christians to encourage them to persevere in their Christian faith. The writer does this by drawing on Jewish history and customs found in the Old Testament. We hear about the role of the Jewish high priest. He alone entered through a curtain into the very special room in the Jewish temple called "the Holy Place." He took with him some blood from animals and sprinkled it there. Blood was a sign of commitment, and to sprinkle it was a prayer for forgiveness.

Note the expression "at the end of the age." This refers to the end of the Old Testament time. Questions being addressed here are:

1. Who is our new High Priest, greater than all previous ones?
2. Where is the new Holy Place, the new sanctuary that he has entered?
3. Who can enter it?

Read the second reading aloud. Reread this Scripture.
What word, phrase, or idea stands out for you?

Exploring Further

1. Where does Jesus ascend to and why?
   Hebrews 9:24
   Hebrews 7:25

2. Compare the following.
   Hebrews 9:2-4, 6-7: How was the sanctuary set up and what is the role of the priest and of the high priest?
   Hebrews 9:11-14, 25-26: How are the sanctuary and Christ's role different?

3. What follows death for mortals in Hebrews 9:27?

4. What will be the purpose of Christ's second coming?
   Hebrews 9:28
   Philippians 3:20-21

5. What is our hope and confidence according to Hebrews 10:19-21?

6. What should our confidence lead to in Hebrews 10:22?

7. What further understanding of assurance of faith, hearts sprinkled clean, and bodies washed in pure water, is given in the following?
   Romans 6:4
   Galatians 2:15-16
   1 Peter 3:20-21

8. Why can we hold fast to our confession of hope?
   Hebrews 10:23
   1 Corinthians 1:9
   1 Corinthians 10:13

9. How are we to live while awaiting the return of Jesus?
   Hebrews 10:24-25
   Acts 2:42

Reflection

1. Over a long period of time, God developed the role of priests, animal sacrifice for sin, the tent, Holy of Holies, and the temple. Then Jesus came as lamb and high priest, sacrificed his life for the forgiveness of sins and entered the heavenly sanctuary. When only the sacrifice of Jesus was effective, what might be some reasons God unfolded this plan over such a long period of time?

2. Jesus came to suffer and die for the forgiveness of sins. His second coming will be to save those who eagerly await him. His coming will be sudden and unexpected. Do you look forward to the second coming with joy, excitement, hesitancy, or fear? Explain. What are practical ways we can prepare and increase our awareness of the reality of the second coming?

3. For the early church faith, baptism, prayer, conversion, repentance, suffering, and service were all interchangeable. When you encountered the risen Jesus your conversion became a way of life that reflected all of these elements. The early church would have been shocked at the idea of faith or baptism or service, etc. What problems arise when we separate these elements of our faith?

Closing Prayer

Lord, we know you are with us always. Help us to live in joyful hope, loving and encouraging one another until you return for us. Amen.

CHAPTER 44
SEVENTH SUNDAY OF EASTER (USA ONLY) YEAR C

OPENING SONG
OPENING PRAYER

Open in prayer and invite everyone to add their own prayer. Close together: "Holy Trinity, may we be one in you that your glory will be evident to the entire world. Through our unity we will make known your love for all. Amen."

REVIEW STUDY GUIDELINES

First Reading   Acts 7:55-60

Setting the Stage

The first reading is from the Acts of the Apostles written by St. Luke about 40 years after the resurrection of Jesus. We hear about the death of the first Christian martyr, St. Stephen. This happens about the year 36 AD. Among those in the crowd that kill him is a man called Saul. Not long after this terrible event, Saul is touched by Jesus and he is changed and becomes one of the greatest apostles of all time—and his name is changed too. He is now known as none other than the great St. Paul! *Through these words we hear how St. Stephen imitated Jesus. Can we do the same?*

Read the first reading aloud. Reread this Scripture.
What word, phrase, or idea stands out for you?

Come to Me

Exploring Further

1. What does Stephen say to the high priest and the Sanhedrin and how do they respond in Acts 7:51-54?

2. What do we know of Stephen from Acts 6:3-6, 8-12, 15?

3. What does Stephen see in Acts 7:55-56?

4. What do the following Scriptures reveal about the glory of God?
   Exodus 24:16
   Matthew 25:31
   John 2:11
   John 11:40-44

5. How does Daniel see the glory of God in Daniel 7:13-14?

6. How do the Sanhedrin respond to Stephen's declaration of seeing the Son of Man in Acts 7:57-58?

7. Where is Stephen dragged to in Acts 7:58a?

8. Where is Jesus killed according to Hebrews 13:12?

9. At whose feet are the cloaks laid while they stone Stephen in Acts 7:58b?

10. What is Saul's attitude toward the persecution and death of believers?
    Acts 22:20
    Acts 26:9-11
    Galatians 1:13

11. How does Saul's perspective change in Acts 9:1-19?

12. What is Stephen's response to those who kill him in Acts 8:59-60?

13. What is Jesus' response to those who kill him in Luke 23:34, 46?

14. How does Stephen's vision and attitude at death fulfill the prayer of Jesus in John 17:20-26, Sunday's gospel?

Seventh Sunday of Easter (USA only) Year C

Reflection

1. The Sanhedrin are stung to the heart and grind their teeth in anger at Stephen's words. How have words of truth stung your heart or made you angry? How did you respond? How have you experienced others reacting in anger to the gospel message? In our culture today, where is there rejection and anger to the gospel message?

2. According to today's readings, the glory of God is manifest through: the presence of God; through belief; through miracles; and through unity with God and other believers. How have you experienced the glory of God in big or small ways? What effect did this experience have on your faith?

3. In the midst of rejection, anger, and being stoned Stephen commended his spirit to God and forgave those who stoned him. In a time of pain and rejection how did you respond? How can we prepare for times of pain and rejection to respond with trust and forgiveness?

Optional Exercise before the second reading. Have each person in the group briefly tell something of their past week or of an event anticipated in the coming week. This could be a time to share a triumph, a trial, or a need.

Second Reading   Revelation 22:12-14, 16-17, 20

Setting the Stage

The second reading is from the book of Revelation written by a certain man named John. The text we hear now gives us some of the very last lines of that book, which describes a vision the author has of Jesus, who rose from the dead about 70 years earlier. *Through these words we hear Jesus describing himself and what he has in store for us.*

Read this reading aloud. Reread this Scripture.
What word, phrase, or idea stands out for you?

Exploring Further

1. What are we to remember in Revelation 22:12?

2. How will rewards be determined?
   Matthew 16:27
   Matthew 25:31-40

Come to Me

    Ezekiel 14:12-14
    Psalm 62:11-12

3. What messianic titles are found in Revelation 22:13, 16b?

4. What beatitude is given in Revelation 22:14?

5. There are seven beatitudes in the book of Revelation. What are the other six?
   Revelation 1:3
   Revelation 14:13
   Revelation 16:15
   Revelation 19:9
   Revelation 20:6
   Revelation 22:7

6. Who calls us in Revelation 22:17a?

7. Who are the bride and bridegroom according to Isaiah 54:5-8?

8. What will take place after the coming of Jesus as described in Revelation 19:7-8?

9. What is promised in Isaiah 55:1-2?

10. How is this fulfilled in Revelation 22:17?

11. What is promised in Revelation 22:20?

12. When will Jesus come and what are we to do while waiting according to Acts 3:19-21?

Reflection

1. We are saved by faith in Jesus Christ. We are rewarded by our deeds. Where do you spend your time? In light of what Jesus will reward, what in your activities should be stopped, started, or stay the same?

2. The seven beatitudes in Revelation are as follows. How are we or how can we be included in the blessed?

   - Blessed is the one who reads aloud the words of the prophecy, and blessed are those who hear and who keep what is written in it, for the time is near;
   - Blessed are the dead who from now on die in the Lord;

Seventh Sunday of Easter (USA only) Year C

- Blessed is the one who stays awake and is clothed, not going about and exposed to shame;
- Blessed are those who are invited to the marriage supper of the Lamb;
- Blessed and holy are those who share in the first resurrection. Over these the second death has no power, but they will be priests of God and of Christ, and they will reign with him a thousand years;
- Blessed is the one who keeps the words of the prophecy of this book;
- Blessed are those who wash their robes, so that they will have the right to the tree of life and may enter the city by the gates.

3. The church is the bride and Jesus is the bridegroom. What image does this bring to your mind? As part of the church, can you picture yourself as the bride of Christ? What do you think the wedding banquet will be like?

4. Do you long for the coming of Jesus or are you anxious or fearful of this event? Explain. How can you make good use of your time while waiting?

Closing Prayer

Lord, thank you for inviting us to "Come." Make us thirsty so we come with great eagerness and joy. Amen.

CHAPTER 45

PENTECOST SUNDAY YEAR C

OPENING SONG
OPENING PRAYER

Open in prayer and invite everyone to add their own prayer. Close together: "Lord, send forth your Spirit and renew the face of the earth. Amen."

REVIEW STUDY GUIDELINES

First Reading — Acts 2:1-11

Setting the Stage

The first reading is from the Acts of the Apostles written by St. Luke who wants to show the meaning of Pentecost. Jews have been celebrating Pentecost for a long time already—it is the celebration of the giving of their Law to Moses on Mount Sinai in the midst of fire and wind. It is here that the people are brought together as one. St. Luke wants to show that in the resurrection of Jesus something similar but more personal and spiritual is experienced by the first Christians.

(Fifty days after the sacrifice of the lamb marking the deliverance of the Hebrews from the Egyptians, the Law is given to the people of Israel on Sinai. Fifty days from the resurrection of Christ after his sacrifice as the true Lamb, the Holy Spirit comes down upon the new Israel.[64])

We hear the ancient names of present-day countries beginning in the east with Iran, coming westward through Turkey and into North Africa, and finally to the capital city of the Roman Empire. The question being addressed is: *what effect does the Spirit have on people who are different?*

Come to Me

Read the first reading aloud. Reread this Scripture.
What word, phrase, or idea stands out for you?

Exploring Further

1. For what festival are the disciples gathered together in one place, according to Acts 2:1?

2. Why do the Israelites celebrate according to Exodus 23:14?

3. What are these three festivals?
   Exodus 23:15
   Leviticus 23:15-16

Note: The fiftieth: from the Greek word for this we have the name "Pentecost." It was also called "the feast of the Seven Weeks," or simply "the feast of Weeks."[65]

Leviticus 23:34 and Deuteronomy 16:3

4. What new thing happened this Pentecost and what did it sound like in Acts 2:2-4?

5. How does Jesus compare a new action of God and wind in John 3:8?

6. Why did Jesus send the Holy Spirit according to John 14:25-26, Sunday's gospel?

7. What condition is attached to receiving the Holy Spirit in John 14:15-17, 23-24?

8. Because of the festival of Pentecost, who was in Jerusalem in Acts 2:5?

9. What drew the crowds' attention according to Acts 2:6?

10. How did they react and why in Acts 2:7-8, 11b-13?

Reflection

1. How have you experienced being empowered by the Holy Spirit to accomplish something?

2. As the wind blows where it will, God's Spirit works in unexpected and surprising ways. Where have you seen, or do you see, the Spirit at work today?

Pope John Paul II singles out five saints as exceptional models of prayer. Four are well known, but who is St. Seraphim of Sarov? St. Seraphim is a Russian saint born in 1759. After his ordination he received permission to live as a hermit in the woods surrounding the monastery, devoting himself to prayer, penance, and spiritual combat. Recalled to the monastery in 1810, Seraphim shut himself up within his cell and continued his solitary life of prayer before his favorite icon. Known as "Our Lady, Joy of All Joys," it represents Mary saying "yes" to God. During the last eight years of Seraphim's life, the fruit of his own repeated "yes" was displayed for all to see. At the Spirit's prompting, Seraphim threw open his cell door. Suddenly his life was transformed into a non-stop ministry of counseling, prayer and healing for thousands who flocked to Sarov from all over Russia. Seraphim was a spiritual counselor with the gift of reading hearts....The monk discerned his friend's unspoken desire to know the true aim of the Christian life. He explained that it consists in acquiring the Holy Spirit through prayer as well as penance and good works done for Christ's sake. God calls everyone to this life of communion with the Trinity, said Seraphim. Seraphim prayed that his friend might experience the Spirit's indwelling presence for himself.... "See, my son, what unspeakable joy the Lord has now granted us!" Seraphim exclaimed, as his friend was swept by waves of light, warmth, heavenly fragrance, and most of all, indescribable joy and peace. "This is what it means to be in the fullness of the Holy Spirit," said the monk. "All that God requires is true faith in himself and his only-begotten Son. In return, the grace of the Holy Spirit is granted abundantly from on High."

Seraphim liked to point out that any outpouring of the Spirit on one person was certain to have a major ripple effect. "Acquire a peaceful spirit and thousands will be saved around you," he used to say. His life invites us to make this discovery of God's loving generosity for ourselves.[66]

3. According to Seraphim, the goal of the Christian life is to acquire the Holy Spirit through prayer, penance, and good works for Christ's sake. Have you ever considered this to be the goal of a Christian? Explain. What might happen if we made this a conscious goal? How is "acquiring" an ongoing process?

4. Where have you witnessed the ripple effects of one person being open to the Holy Spirit?

Optional Exercise before the second reading. Have each person in the group briefly tell something of their past week or of an event anticipated in the coming week. This could be a time to share a triumph, a trial, or a need.

Come to Me

Second Reading   Romans 8:8-17

Setting the Stage

The second reading is from the letter of St. Paul written about 25 years after the resurrection of Jesus to the Christians living in Rome. Through St. Paul, God our Father tells us that the Holy Spirit makes Jesus present to us. The question is: *what are the results, the implications of the Spirit of Christ being in us?*

Read the second reading aloud. Reread this Scripture.
What word, phrase, or idea stands out for you?

Exploring Further

1. What four things about the flesh are mentioned in Romans 8:7-9?

2. What results when Christ lives within you?
    Romans 8:10-11
    Romans 6:4, 8-11

3. What are the fruits of living by the Spirit and of living by the flesh?
    Romans 8:12-14
    Galatians 5:19-25
    Galatians 6:7-8

4. What are some of the things the Spirit does for us?
    Romans 8:14-17
    Romans 8:26
    John 16:8
    John 16:13
    Matthew 10:20
    Ephesians 1:13-14

Reflection

1. How can I tell if I am living by the flesh or living by the Spirit at any given moment?

2. Where in our society do you see fruits of living by the flesh and living by the Spirit?

3. God's Spirit makes us children that cry "Abba;" the Spirit guides us in truth and gives us understanding of God's word, helps us overcome our areas of weakness, convicts us of sin and leads us to repentance, directs us in serving the Lord, leads us in sanctification, and guarantees our place in heaven and much more. When in your life have you experienced the Spirit working in one or more of these ways?

Closing Prayer

Come Holy Spirit, fill our hearts and kindle in us the fire of your love. Amen.

CHAPTER 46

TRINITY SUNDAY YEAR C

OPENING SONG
OPENING PRAYER

Open in prayer and invite everyone to add their own prayer. Close together: "Father thank you for sending your Word made flesh to redeem us and your Spirit to teach us and make us holy. As we come to glimpse this mystery, may we worship you, one God in three Persons; the Father, Son, and Holy Spirit. Amen."

REVIEW STUDY GUIDELINES

First Reading   Proverbs 8:22-31

Setting the Stage

The first reading is from the book of Proverbs. This Old Testament book is put together over a very long period of time and reaches its present format about 400 to 500 years before Jesus. Thus, the book's concept of the world is very different from ours. We shall hear a beautiful description of the Wisdom of God as a separate, distinct person. (The apostles would later come to see these words as being a prediction of Jesus.)[67] Listen to the colorful style and put on your poet's hat! This is literature at its best. *We hear about the One who is at work in all of creation.*

Read the first reading aloud. Reread this Scripture.
What word, phrase, or idea stands out for you?

Come to Me

Exploring Further

1. How is wisdom presented in Proverbs 8:22-23?

2. How is wisdom more fully revealed in John 1:1-3?

3. What attributes are given to wisdom?
   Wisdom 9:9
   Sirach 1:6-10 (or verses 5-8.)(See appendix one.)

4. How is creation planned and executed in Proverbs 8:24-29?

5. How does wisdom relate to others in Proverbs 8:30-31?

6. What do we discover about "delight?"
   Psalm 35:4, 9-10
   Psalm 119:13-16, 24
   Psalm 37:4
   Isaiah 58:13-14

7. What do the following verses say about God's delight?
   Isaiah 5:7a
   Isaiah 65:18-19
   Zephaniah 3:17

8. What is a prudent response to wisdom according to Proverbs 8:32-34?

9. What are the consequences of how we respond to wisdom in Proverbs 8:35-36?

10. What is Jesus called in 1 Corinthians 1:24-25?

11. Who will continue to guide us in wisdom in John 16:12-15, Sunday's gospel?

Reflection

1. What attributes of wisdom discussed in this study appeal to you?

2. How do you seek wisdom, and is seeking wisdom a priority in your life? Explain.

3. If wisdom delights in being in the presence of God and delights in the human race, what are ways we can imitate this?

Trinity Sunday Year C

4. The Trinity is a community. The body of Christ is a community where relationships with God, self, and others must be maintained. Hermits and contemplatives have time for self and God. How can they maintain the balance in relationship to others? An example would be St. Therese of Lisseux, who was a contemplative and is now the patron saint of missionaries. How can people in the business of life balance these three crucial relationships of God, self and others?

Optional Exercise before the second reading. Have each person in the group briefly tell something of their past week or of an event anticipated in the coming week. This could be a time to share a triumph, a trial, or a need.

Second Reading   Romans 5:1-5

Setting the Stage

The second reading, from the letter of St. Paul to the Christians of Rome, is specially chosen for this feast of Trinity Sunday because all three Persons of the Blessed Trinity are mentioned. An especially important reminder is this: for St. Paul and generally throughout the New Testament, the name of God is used to refer only to God the Father.[68] Since we have been given the gift of faith, we can be happy about two things, or as St. Paul puts it, we can boast about two things. *What are they?*

Read the second reading aloud. Reread this Scripture.
What word, phrase, or idea stands out for you?

Exploring Further

1. What does justification by faith bring us according to Romans 5:1?

2. What have we gained and of what do we boast according to Romans 5:2?

3. What is the basis of our hope according to 1 Peter 1:21?

4. Amazingly, what else can we boast of according to Romans 5:3a?

5. What do the difficulties of life teach us according to Romans 5:3b-4?

6. In our sufferings, what is helpful to know from 2 Corinthians 12:9-10?

7. What attitude is recommended and why?
   James 1:2-4
   1 Peter 4:13-14

8. Why will our hope not leave us disappointed according to Romans 5:5?

9. What is the proof of the Spirit poured into our hearts in Galatians 4:6?

Reflection

1. What images do "pouring down" or "poured into" bring to mind? Romans 5:5 states "the love of God has been poured into our hearts." Does applying the above images help you picture God's love as abundant? Why or why not?

2. Can you think of a time you had hope in the midst of hardship? Explain.

3. 'The Trinity is a community. When we live and worship together in community, we imitate the Trinity. Picture a lawn with dandelions. Dandelions have long roots and spread easily. Yet most of us persevere in working to remove dandelions from our lawn. Sin within the community is like dandelions. Yet we continue with perseverance and hope to grow together in love. A common reason people often stop worshipping with a church community is that they were hurt and have experienced our shortcomings as individuals or as a community.[69] Which of today's Scriptures—"our hope being in God;" "we learn through life's hardships;" "in our weakness we can rely on Christ's power;" "the Holy Spirit infuses God's love into our hearts;" may be of help to you when you are hurt by the community or deeply aware of the community's shortcomings? Explain.

Closing Prayer

Lord God, we worship you, a Trinity of Persons, one eternal God. Glory be to the Father and to the Son and to the Holy Spirit: to God who is, who was, and who is to come. Amen.

CHAPTER 47

BODY AND BLOOD OF CHRIST
YEAR C

OPENING SONG
OPENING PRAYER

Open in prayer and invite everyone to add their own prayer. Close together: "Father, we thank you for sending us our high priest, Jesus Christ, who nourishes us, blesses us, and rescues us from the grave. Amen."

REVIEW STUDY GUIDELINES

First Reading Genesis 14:18-20

Setting the Stage

The first reading is from the book of Genesis. We hear of an event in the life of Abraham who lives about 1800 BC. His name is originally Abram. In the following reading we see what happens to him on his way home after rescuing his nephew Lot who has been kidnapped. We hear a strange name: Melchizedek. He is king of Salem (Jerusalem is also known as Salem), and he is also a priest of a religion in Palestine at the time.[70] Today's psalm response after this reading will speak about him as well. Since in the book of Genesis there is no mention of him before or after his meeting with Abraham, he becomes a symbol of another "Priest" who has no beginning and will have no end. Notice what kind of food and drink he uses to bless Abraham; a kind of prediction of the holy meal to be prepared for us by this "Other Priest"!

Read the first reading aloud. Reread this Scripture.
What word, phrase, or idea stands out for you?

Come to Me

Exploring Further

1. What happens to Abraham's nephew Lot and how does Abraham respond in Genesis 14:13-16?

2. How does God rescue?
   2 Samuel 22:18-20
   Psalm 107:19-20
   Colossians 1:13-14

3. Who greets Abraham on his return from victory in Genesis 14:17-18a?

4. What is similar between Melchizedek and Jesus?
   Genesis 14:18
   Psalm 110:4
   Hebrews 7:1-3

There are three main points of resemblance between Melchizedek, the prophetic type, and Christ who fulfilled this prophecy: both are kings as well as priests, both offer bread and wine to God, and both have their priesthood directly from God and not through Aaron, since neither belongs to the tribe of Levi.[71]

5. What does Melchizedek give Abraham in Genesis 14:18-20?

6. What offering do the disciples give Jesus in Luke 9:13-15?

7. What blessing does Jesus give this small offering and with what results, according to Luke 9:16-17, Sunday's gospel?

8. What blessing does Jesus give and with what results in Mathew 26:26-28?

9. How does God bless?
   Genesis 1:27, 28
   Genesis 12:2-3

A blessing is an effective and irrevocable word which, even when pronounced by a man, produces the effect which it expresses, since God confers the blessing.[72]

10. What blessings are given in the following Scriptures?
    Genesis 28:1-4
    Psalm 67:1-2
    Psalm 128:5

11. How can we bless God?
    Exodus 18:10
    Deuteronomy 8:10
    Luke 1:68-69
    Ephesians 1:3
    1 Peter 1:3

12. What does Abraham do in Genesis 14:20b?

13. What is said regarding tithing in the following Scriptures?
    Numbers 18:25-29
    2 Chronicles 31:4-5
    Malachi 3:8-10

Reflection

1. Abraham rescues Lot from captivity. God has rescued us from captivity to sin and death. In your life, where has God rescued you? How have you moved from spiritual captivity to freedom?

2. How have you experienced blessings from others in your life? Who have you blessed? How important is blessing our children, parents, others? How does Jesus bless us?

3. The Israelites were expected to bring a tenth of the best of their crops and livestock as an offering to the Lord and to support the priests. Does God expect us to tithe today? What is your experience with tithing? How can we become generous givers?

4. In today's gospel the crowd was large and the disciples only had a little to give. Jesus blessed and multiplied their offering. What large needs do you see are needed in your family, community, country, and world? What little do you have to give? Where have you given the "little" of your time, talent, service, or income in the name of Jesus and with prayer, and God did something good with it?

Come to Me

Second Reading   1 Corinthians 11:23-26

Setting the Stage

The next reading is from the first letter that St. Paul writes to the church in Corinth, Greece about 25 years after the resurrection of Jesus. He is in southwestern Turkey when some Corinthians tell him about their problems, one of them being the drunken and selfish behavior of some at Mass. Through these words, God our Father speaks to us on this very special day about the greatest of all the sacraments. He answers the following questions: *From whom does the Mass come? What do we proclaim and celebrate here?*

Read the second reading aloud. Reread this Scripture.
What word, phrase, or idea stands out for you?

Exploring Further

1. What does Jesus do on the night of his betrayal in 1 Corinthians 11:23-25?

2. In doing this what does Jesus institute according to Luke 22:20?

3. What is the old covenant that prefigures this covenant in Exodus 12:3, 7, 11-13?

4. What is foretold in Jeremiah 31:31-34?

5. Who is the mediator of this new covenant in Hebrews 8:6-9?

6. How is a covenant ratified in the Old Testament according to Exodus 24:7-8?

7. How is the new covenant ratified in Hebrews 9:12-15?

8. What is the need of the people and how does Jesus meet this need in Luke 9:11-17, Sunday's gospel?

9. What do we proclaim when we participate in this new covenant?
   1 Corinthians 11:26
   1 Corinthians 15:3-4

10. What is happening at the Eucharistic gatherings in 1 Corinthians 11:17-21?

11. What does participation in the Eucharist require in 1 Corinthians 11:27-31?

Reflection

1. How have you experienced Jesus refreshing, healing, and nourishing you?

2. At every Eucharist we proclaim Christ has died, Christ is risen, and Christ will come again. Why is this threefold remembrance important? How is each statement relative to your life today?

3. The Passover was on the eve of the Israelites' freedom from slavery in Egypt and the doors marked with blood were spared the death of their firstborn. At the Eucharist we are receiving our own freedom from sin and celebrating the birth of new life. How can we grow in awareness of this truth and avoid apathy as we partake in the Eucharist? How do you understand your freedom from slavery to sin and rebirth of new life?

4. To participate in the Eucharist belief, unity and a clear conscience are necessary. Do you believe you are receiving the body and blood of Jesus? Are you in unity with the church? Do you have relationships that need reconciling? Are you free of grave sin before partaking in the Eucharist? Why are these conditions necessary?

Closing Prayer

Lord, in your precious blood we find life and in your resurrection we have the hope of eternal life. Thank you for healing, refreshing, and nourishing us until you come again. Amen.

APPENDIX ONE
DEUTEROCANONICAL BOOKS/APOCRYPHA

The following books are considered the Deuterocanonical or Apocrypha: Tobit, Judith, Sirach (Ecclesiasticus), Wisdom, 1 & 2 Maccabees, Baruch, and parts of Daniel.

Among Christians it was apparently not until the fourth century that the issue of canonicity (to recognize officially as inspired books to be included in the Bible) of these books arose.

In 1546 at the Council of Trent the Roman Catholic Church officially declared these books to be sacred and canonical and to be accepted "with equal devotion and reverence."

At the time of the Reformation Martin Luther did not regard these books as Scripture but as "useful and good for reading." In his German translation of the Bible he placed them at the end of the Old Testament with the superscription "Apocrypha." Protestants generally continued this practice in their translations of the Bible.

Catholics speak of these books as "Deuterocanonical" to indicate that their canonical status as Scripture was settled later than that of the Protocanonical books. Others usually refer to these books as Apocrypha.[73]

For this Bible study I suggest you bring a Bible that includes the Apocrypha as there are some readings from this section each year. If you have a Catholic Bible, these books will automatically be included. If you have a Protestant Bible, the Apocrypha will not usually be included unless it states "with Apocryphal Books."

APPENDIX TWO
DEFININTION OF THE WORD "WORLD" AS USED IN SCRIPTURE

The word "*World*" is used in three ways in Scripture:

1. "*World*" as meaning physical creation. It is used in this way in Genesis.[74]
2. "*World*" meaning all that is hostile to God; all that stands in enmity with God. Love of the world reflects attachment to what is transitory. Love of God brings Christians into relationship with what "remains" forever.[75] It is used this way in 1, 2, and 3 John.
3. "*World*" used to mean people. It is used this way in John 3:16, "For God so loved the world that he sent his only Son, so that every one who believes in him may not perish but may have eternal life."

ENDNOTES

1. *Catechism of the Catholic Church* (Publication Service, Canadian Conference of Catholic Bishops, 1994) #2459, #2460.
2. Reprinted from *The Word Among Us,* September 2003, p.34, The Word Among Us Press, 9639 Dr. Perry Road, Suite 126, Ijamsville, Maryland, 21754, www.wordamongus.org. Used with permission.
3. *Catechism of the Catholic Church,* (Publications Service, Canadian Conference of Catholic Bishops, 1994) #2452.
4. Ibid., #1626, #1628.
5. www.stdanielclarkston.org/annulment.htm.
6. *Life Application Bible,* NRSV Tyndale House Publishers, Inc.,1990) footnote Hebrews 4.12.
7. *The New Jerusalem Bible* (Garden City, New York, Doubleday & Company, Inc. 1985) Jer. 30, note a; New Oxford Annotated Bible with Apocrypha, NRSV(Oxford University Press, 1991) Jeremiah 31:7-11, note.
8. *The Handy Bible Dictionary & Concordance* (Zondervan Corporation, 1983) p. 100.
9. *The New Jerusalem Bible* (Garden City,New York, Doubleday & Company, Inc. 1985) footnote Heb. 10b.
10. *The New Jerome Biblical Commentary* (New Jersey, Prentice Hall, 1990) pages 997-999.
11. *New Oxford Annotated Bible with Apocrypha,* NRSV (Oxford University Press, 1991) page 346.
12. *The New Jerusalem Bible* (Garden City,New York, Doubleday & Company, Inc.1985) page 2039.
13. *New Oxford Annotated Bible with Apocrypha,* NRSV (Oxford University Press, 1991) Rev. 7:4 note.
14. *The Jerome Biblical Commentary* (New Jersey, Prentice Hall, 1968) Rev 7:3, p.478.
15. *New Oxford Annotated Bible with Apocrypha,* NRSV (Oxford University Press, 1991) Rev. 7:3, p. 478.
16. *The New Jerusalem Bible* (Garden City,New York, Doubleday & Company, Inc.1985) Rev 4.4, note h.
17. *Catechism of the Catholic Church,* (Publications Service, Canadian Conference of Catholic Bishops 1994) #1030.

18. *New Oxford Annotated Bible with Apocrypha,* NRSV (Oxford University Press, 1991) 1 Cor 15 note page 246.
19. Pope Paul IX, *Dogmatic Constitution on the Church,* Lumen Gentium, 1964 Vat. II, ch.7, #49, 268.
20. *Catechism of the Catholic Church,* (Publications Service, Canadian Conference of Catholic Bishops 1994) #997,#998, #999.
21. *New Oxford Annotated Bible with Apocrypha,* NRSV (Oxford University Press, 1991) Ezekiel 47:8, note.
22. N. Gumbel, *Questions of Life* (Cook Communications Ministries, 1993, 1996) P.129.
23. *Catechism of the Catholic Church* (Publications Service, Canadian Conference of Catholic Bishops 1994) # 2563.
24. *Life Application Bible* NRSV (Tyndale House Publishers, Inc. 1990) footnote 1 K 17.1.
25. P. Takeda in "Living with Christ" *Sunday Missal,* Jubilee Edition, 2000 (Ottawa, Novalis Saint Paul University, 1999) p. 521 Reproduced with permission. Website: www.novalis.ca.
26. *Life Application Bible,* NRSV (Tyndale House Publishers, Inc. 1990) footnote Heb. 10.14.
27. Fr. B. Inglis, homily. Used with permission.
28. *Life Application Bible,* NRSV (Tyndale House Publishers. Inc., 1990) footnote Mi. 5.1,5.1ff.
29. *Catechism of the Catholic Church* (Publications Service, Canadian Conference of Catholic Bishops 1994) #1269,#1270.
30. Ibid., #1170.
31. *The New Jerusalem Bible* (Garden City, New York, Doubleday & Company, Inc.1985) Is. 1:26n.
32. Ibid., footnote Ez. 7c.
33. *Life Application Bible* NRSV, (Tyndale House Publishers. Inc., 1989) Lk. footnote 4:16.
34. *New Jerusalem Bible* (Garden City, New York, Doubleday & Company, Inc. 1985) "Introduction to the Prophets," p. 1170.
35. Ibid., footnote Jr. 1c.
36. Ibid., 1 Cor. 12:10, note g.
37. *The New Jerome Bible Commentary* (New Jersey, Prentice Hall, 1990) p. 199-200, p. 811.
38. Ibid., p. 811.
39. *The New American Bible,* (Catholic Book Publishing Company, 1992) footnote Is. 6:1ff.
40. Ibid., footnote Is. 6:7.
41. Pope Paul Vl, "Apostolic Exhortation On Evangelization in the Modern World," #13, #15.
42. *New Oxford Annotated Bible with Apocrypha,* NRSV (Oxford University Press, 1991) "Introduction to Jr," p. 960.
43. John Connelly, Western Catholic Reporter. Used with permission.
44. *New Oxford Annotated Bible with Apocrypha,* NRSV (Oxford University Press, 1991) 1 Cor 15:1, note p. 245.
45. Ibid., 1 Cor 15, note p. 245.
46. Ibid., Rm 10:13, note.

ENDNOTES

47. F. Van Gennip in "Living in Christ" *Sunday Missal,* 2000-2001 (Ottawa, Novalis, Saint Paul University, 2000) p.185 Reproduced with permission. Website: www.novalis.ca.
48. *The New Jerusalem Bible* (Garden City, New York, Doubleday & Company, Inc.1985) footnote Ex. 19e.
49. *Life Application Bible,* NRSV (Tyndale House Publishers, Inc., 1989) footnote Ex. 3:14,15.
50. *Harper Collins Study Bible* NRSV (Harper Collins Publishers, 1989) footnote 1 Cor. 10:4.
51. M. Dougherty in "Living with Christ" *Sunday Missal,* 2003-2004 (Ottawa, Novalis, Saint Paul University, 2003) p. 207 Reproduced with permission. Website: www.novalis.ca.
52. *The New Jerusalem Bible* (Garden City, New York, Doubleday & Company, Inc. 1985) footnote Rm 1h.
53. Archbishop F. Sheen, *Suffering, Death & Resurrection* (audiotape by St. Joseph Communications Inc., 1993) tape7.
54. *The New Jerusalem Bible* (Garden City, New York, Doubleday & Company, Inc. 1985) Ph. 1:5, note d.
55. Ibid., Ph. 2:10, note n, Rv. 5:3, note c.
56. Ibid., Rv. 1:13 footnote n.
57. Ibid., footnote Ac 2n.
58. Ibid., Rv. 5, note h.
59. Ibid., Rv. 7 note g.
60. *The Handy Bible Dictionary & Concordance* (Zondervan Corporation, 1983) definition p. 52.
61. *Harper Collins Study Bible,* NRSV (Harper Collins Publishers, 1989) footnote Rv. 7.16.
62. *Catechism of the Catholic Church* (Publications Service, Canadian Conference of Catholic Bishops 1994) #796.
63. Reprinted from L. Zanchettin, Acts, *A Devotional Commentary,* 2001, p.131, The Word Among Us Press, 9639 Dr. Perry Road, Suite 126, Ijamsville, Maryland, 21754, www.wordamongus.org. Used with permission.
64. Ibid., p. 31.
65. *St. Joseph Edition of the New American Bible* (New York, Catholic Book Publishing Co. 1986) note Lv 23:16.
66. Reprinted from *The Word Among Us,* Easter Edition 2003, p. 61-65, The Word Among Us Press, 9639 Dr. Perry Road, Suite 126, Ijamsville, Maryland, 21754, www.wordamongus.org. Used with permission.
67. *The New Jerusalem Bible* (Garden City, New York, Doubleday & Company, Inc. 1985) Pr. 8:22 note c.
68. Ibid., Rm. 9:15, note d.
69. Fr. Brian's Homily (used with permission).
70. *New Oxford Annotated Bible with Apocrypha,* NRSV (Oxford University Press, 1991) Gn 14:19-20 note.
71. *St. Joseph Edition of the New American Bible,* (New York, Catholic Book Publishing Co. 1970) note Ps. 110:4.

72. *The New Jerusalem Bible,* (Garden City, New York, Doubleday & Company, Inc. 1985) footnote Gn. 14h.
73. *Good News Bible* (American Bible Society, 1979) "Introduction to the Deutercanonical/Apocryphal Books."
74. *New Jerome Biblical* Commentary (New Jersey, Prentice Hall, 1990) 82:44.
75. Ibid., 47:32 and 62:21.

To order additional copies of this title call:
1-877-421-READ (7323)
or please visit our web site at
www.pleasantwordbooks.com

Printed in the United States
63596LVS00005B/35-50